4TH EDITION

THE ULTIMATE
SALES
LETTER

4TH EDITION

THE ULTIMATE
SALES
LETTER

ATTRACT NEW CUSTOMERS.
BOOST YOUR SALES.

DAN S. KENNEDY

Author of the *BusinessWeek* Bestseller *No B.S. Business Success*

Avon, Massachusetts

Published by Adams Business,
an imprint of Adams Media, a division of F+W Media, Inc.
57 Littlefield Street, Avon, MA 02322. U.S.A.
www.adamsmedia.com

ISBN 10: 1-4405-1141-1
ISBN 13: 978-1-4405-1141-7
eISBN 10: 1-4405-1190-X
eISBN 13: 978-1-4405-1190-5

Printed in the United States of America.

10   9   8   7

Library of Congress Cataloging-in-Publication Data
is available from the publisher.

This publication is designed to provide accurate and authoritative information with regard to the subject matter covered. It is sold with the understanding that the publisher is not engaged in rendering legal, accounting, or other professional advice. If legal advice or other expert assistance is required, the services of a competent professional person should be sought.

—From a *Declaration of Principles* jointly adopted by a Committee of the American Bar Association and a Committee of Publishers and Associations

Many of the designations used by manufacturers and sellers to distinguish their product are claimed as trademarks. Where those designations appear in this book and Adams Media was aware of a trademark claim, the designations have been printed with initial capital letters.

This book is available at quantity discounts for bulk purchases.

For information, please call 1-800-289-0963.

What Can You Expect from *The Ultimate Sales Letter*?

Since its first publication in 1990, this book has inspired and guided tens of thousands of people in diverse businesses and sales activities in creating and using "the ultimate sales letter." Here are a few of their comments:

> "One sales letter campaign developed from your instructions has actually produced so much business for my practice that I no longer have marketing needs. I only have trouble handling all the clients!"
> **—Harry Williams**
> Attorney, Illinois

> "I have invested well over $200,000.00 having Dan Kennedy write ads and sales letters for me. Getting an inside look at his method in this book is the bargain of the century."
> **—Rory Fatt**
> Restaurant Marketing Systems, Inc., Vancouver BC

"Carefully following the instructions in *The Ultimate Sales Letter*, I put together a long letter for the purpose of securing appointments with top decision-makers in my industry. In over twenty years in this business, I've never sent anything longer than a one-page letter, and frankly, I doubted your approach. But this time, instead of fighting through secretaries and making follow-up call after follow-up call, these prospects were calling me. So far, I've written over $50,000.00 in new business from mailing only 2,500 letters."

—John Cummings
Michigan

"I've been a marketing director for nearly ten years. I know quite a bit. My promotions pulled results; bosses and clients loved me. But I was not aware of how much I didn't know! If Dan Kennedy required my next-born child in exchange for the information he has given, I'd pay to have a reversal of my tubal ligation."

—Bridget Campbell
Marketing Director, Idaho

And from Down Under . . .

"I have been a keen student of yours for close to ten years. More than any other direct-marketing expert on the planet, it is your tactics, strategies, and principles that have directly contributed to my success. From a Dan Kennedy neophyte to Kennedy expert, my achievements, including being CEO of Australia's twenty-ninth fastest-growing company and achieving rank of Australia's thirty-ninth richest young entrepreneur (per *Business Review Weekly* magazine), can be attributed to your teachings. Our products are now in every department store in the United States, the GNC stores, and we are looking forward to exponential growth this year."

—Peter Nicholas
Naturopathica/Skin Doctors Cosmeceuticals
Sydney, Australia

"There have been great copywriters in the past twenty-five years that are without peer. After the death of Eugene Schwarz, there are only three left living, and you, Dan Kennedy, are one of the three! Your copywriting advice, like that in *The Ultimate Sales Letter*, has helped me write copy that makes more than $60 million a year. You are my secret weapon."

—Sonia Amoroso
Naturopathica/Skin Doctors Cosmeceuticals
Sydney, Australia

Contents

You've Got the Power

Katie Yeakle

Turning words into profits. That's what sales letters do.

If you're a business owner, sales letters find new customers for you and persuade them to give you a chance. They keep your existing customers connected to you and buying more. And, they bring back customers who have left the fold and encourage them to buy from you again.

Understand how sales letters work and you'll have the power to create a successful business . . . and the life you want to live.

By the time you're done with this book, you'll have that understanding. Plus, you'll know how to recognize "fatal flaws" in letters written for you . . . you'll know how to get the most out of every sales letter you mail . . . and you'll know how to speak about sales copy in a meaningful and efficient way.

If, however, you picked up this book because you like to write, I have great news for you too.

You now have in your hands a ticket for living "the writer's life."

Just imagine. . . . You can make more money than many doctors and lawyers make—just by writing simple, conversational letters like the ones you'll be studying in the pages ahead. For over a decade now, American Writers & Artists, Inc. (AWAI), the organization I'm proud to have helped create, has been showing folks who are sick of the rat race, or who simply want to make more money, how writing sales letters (aka "copywriting") is the easiest and most fun way to start living a better and more stress-free life.

The ability to persuade via the written word, which is what you're about to learn how to do, is a skill that is, and always will be, in very high demand. Plus . . . since as a copywriter you own your business, you can work where you want . . . when you want. You're in total control.

And even though AWAI has done a good job "spreading the word" about the huge demand for people who can write sales letters, more letters are still needed.

Since the emergence of the Internet as a proven and vital marketing vehicle, the demand for letters, and people who can write them, has gone through the roof!

In the pages ahead, you're going to learn how to harness the power of these simple letters from one of the most successful and highly paid sales letter writers in the world, Dan Kennedy.

As Dan tells you right up front, "Don't be intimidated by the idea or process of writing. There's no magic or genius or Harvard degree required."

In *The Ultimate Sales Letter*, Dan gives you his system for writing and maximizing the power of a sales letter. You'll know how to attract customers and how to boost sales. He gives you his best secrets, techniques, and tactics for profiting from what he calls "the most versatile sales tool of all."

By the time you're done reading *The Ultimate Sales Letter*, you'll have the power to transform your business and your life.

—Katie Yeakle
AWAI's Executive Director
www.awaionline.com

Part 1

Before You Write a Word

What to Do Before You Start Writing

Take a deep breath. Relax.

If you're a pro copywriter for whom this book is a reference, welcome—you will find a solid checkup of your methods here, and maybe a trick or two or three to add to your tool bag.

But if you're *not* a pro writer, as the vast majority of people who have found and used this book in its prior editions over twenty years aren't, you have nothing to fear here! This book is for you.

I am convinced that just about anybody can learn to craft very effective sales letters. I have no opinion one way or the other about your ability to write the next Great American Novel, a cookbook, a children's storybook, or a Broadway play. (I've written a country-and-western song: "I Love My Wife but I Forgot Where I Live." But that's another story.) I do have great confidence in your ability to write a successful sales letter, for two basic reasons.

First, you presumably know more about your business, product, service, and customer than anybody else. Getting that understanding is the hard part. Writing with that understanding is easy.

When I or some other freelancer is brought in to write sales letters, we have to do our best to acquire that understanding before we can even begin writing. That takes a lot of time and effort and energy, and there's still no way we can get exactly the same full understanding, the same intuitive insights from experience, that you must have in your chosen business.

This is a tremendous advantage and you, my friend, possess it.

Second, my own background tells me that just about anybody can learn to do this. I am a high-school, not a college, graduate. I did not go to work in the mailroom of some ad agency and learn the trade of copywriting from experienced, seasoned pros while pulling myself up the corporate ladder. In fact, I got my first paid copywriting assignment while still a senior in high school and opened my own ad agency two years later, with no relevant experience or education behind me. I just did the same things you can do:

1. I got books like this one, devoured them, kept them handy, and used them as guides. I sure wish there had been a book exactly like this one, with a step-by-step system, but there were, and are, plenty of other good ones.
2. I used my own insight, intuition, powers of observation, and common sense.
3. I translated what I knew (and what I kept discovering) about selling and communicating in person to the task of selling and communicating in print.
4. I built up huge "idea files"—samples of ads, mailings, and sales letters. These are called "swipe files" by pros, and that is exactly what they are used for—to swipe ideas

from. You do not need much creativity to write letters; you only need to be adept at recycling and reorganizing ideas, themes, words, and phrases.

Despite of my lack of formal education or training in this field, I've developed literally thousands of print ads, sales letters, direct-mail campaigns, and online campaigns for hundreds of clients, and more than 90 percent have been successful. Even though I am paid from $50,000.00 to $150,000.00 to as much as $2 million plus royalties for such a campaign, over 85 percent of all clients who use me enlist my services again. Some continuously. Many of my sales letters have been tested against established successes written by other top professional copywriters and I've won these "beat the best" competitions almost every time. I do not tell you all this to brag; I tell it so that you will realize that you can do it, too. I'm self-taught. You can be self-taught.

Also, for most of your purposes, you do not need the same skill level that I or other top, professional copywriters have painstakingly developed. In most situations I work in, I'm putting together sales letters that will compete against other sales letters written by other top pros, but you will more likely be competing in an environment where top-flight pro copywriters do not prowl.

I have been motivated—and urge you to be motivated—by what another top copywriter, John Francis Tighe, says frequently: "In the land of the blind, the one-eyed man is king."

Since this book was first published, I've received literally thousands of "success stories" from people in every imaginable business or sales career who have used this book as their guide, put together a sales letter from scratch, and achieved desirable and profitable results. Some have gone on to great proficiency. Several have become consultants and copywriters.

I recognize that a large part of your success will depend on your confidence to do something. The mechanics are all here for you. But ultimately you have to go from your first read of this book to the act of following its steps, getting sales letters prepared, and into the mail.

Here are some general ideas that will help you get started:

1. Don't be intimidated by the idea or process of writing. There's no magic or genius or Harvard degree required.
2. Recognize the value and power of your unique understanding of your business, products, services, and customers. You may find it useful to build reference lists or stacks of 3-by-5-inch cards—"What I Know about Our Customers . . . about Our Product . . ." and so on.
3. Assemble and organize ideas and samples in a "swipe file"; assemble and organize good reference materials.
4. Think *selling*. If you have successful sales experience—terrific! Writing a sales letter is much more akin to getting down on the living room floor with Ma, Pa, the kids, and the dog and selling a vacuum cleaner than anything else. If you don't have a "selling mentality," get one! Get some good books on selling. (See my website, *www.dankennedy.com*, and this publisher's website, *www.adamsmedia.com*, for some ideas.) Never forget that a sales letter is a sales presentation in print.
5. Write. Don't worry about writing a letter from start to finish. Just write blocks of copy and stack them up. A lot of great sales letters are eventually put together with

       scissors and tape (or by cutting and pasting on the computer). Write!

6. Avoid perfectionism. In most businesses, for most purposes, you don't need a perfect sales letter to get good results. If you follow the guidelines in this book, have something worthwhile to offer, and understand your customer, you may not put together the perfect sales letter, but I'll bet you will put together one that works.

Many people believe that the great, persuasive sales letter writers just sit down at their computers and let the priceless prose flow! I have known two or three who can do this, but most do not. Most professional sales letter writers give themselves the advantage of careful, thorough preparation, and you should, too.

Remember, **the more you write, the easier it will get.** Just about everything you do easily now was once difficult to do. From fear to confidence, difficult to easy, incompetent to competent—that's a movement we repeat over and over again throughout our lives. It's the process that gives life meaning, that prevents boredom, burnout, and depression. It's good for you! It builds healthy self-esteem, which prevents unhealthy addictions and destructive behavior. Gaining new competence in any skill, such as writing sales letters, automatically enhances your confidence in all other areas. In short, you're going to find the ability to craft effective sales letters to be a major asset personally and for your company.

Just as I am convinced that anybody can master the craft of writing effective sales letters, I am also convinced that a sales letter can be developed to sell anything.

My clients prove it. Darin Garman sells heartland-of-America apartment building and commercial property investments sight unseen to investors in California, New Jersey, even Japan, with letters sent from his office in Cedar Rapids, Iowa. Alan Reed at Reed's Dairy built his home delivery clientele from 300 homes to nearly 3,000 homes with sales letters (and postcards). In B2B (business-to-business), Dr. Chris Tomshack sells franchises to chiropractic physicians with sales letters. You name the product or service, and I can show you examples of it being sold successfully and profitably with sales letters. By the way, although I got them started one way or another, Darin, Alan, and Chris write their own sales letters, each generating millions of dollars a year in income for their businesses by doing so. You can too. For any product, service, or business.

My old friend Gary Halbert said, "There's no problem for which a great sales letter can't be the solution!"

Now you hold in your hands a simple, yet powerful, step-by-step process you can use to experience the power of sales letters for yourself. Go get 'em!

Here is the first page of a multipage letter Darin wrote for one of his properties—it is typical of the letters he writes for different properties. Following it, a copy of the order form: yes, investors fax in credit card info or FedEx in checks to invest, just as if buying a pair of shoes from a mail-order catalog!

Exhibit #1A First Page of Sales Letter

THIS EXCLUSIVE REPORT IS ONLY INTENDED FOR PERSONS REQUESTING INFORMATION ON THE SHADOWOOD APARTMENTS...

After 'hanging out' with these people for over 10 years I have figured out...

"Why The Shadowood Apartments Is The Kind Of Apartment Property That My Most Successful Apartment Property Investors Put Their Money Into– And How *YOU* Can Join Them"

For those apartment investors and owners that want to earn as much money in a short period of time there is one thing that has to be present. One thing above all else to get you the profits quicker than the average investor. I mean average investors get average results don't they?

What Is The One 'Thing', This "Trump Card Secret" of Successful Apartment Investors?

<u>A Motivated Seller!!</u>

Dear Friend:

You know how is goes. Many times you may be able to find those properties that seem to look "OK", but, you then find out the seller IS NOT motivated to sell the property.

A Heartland Of America Apartment Property Like The Shadowood Apartments Can Build Your Wealth, Predictably, Without Any Management Needed On Your Part.

The owner has it on the market and if it does sell for the price they are looking for, GREAT, if not, no big deal.

You Want to Make Sure You Do Everything You Can To Work With A Motivated Owner! And I Have A Motivated Owner Ready To Work With You...

If you don't work with a motivated owner it is difficult to negotiate great prices and terms that can build your wealth as quickly as possible. Or, in other words you will be dealing with the slow way to wealth, the average way.

The Faster, Less Stressful, Management Free Way To Apartment Property Wealth— The Shadowood Apartments Fit This Bill To A "T" - ESPECIALLY If You Have Been Wanting To Get Into Apartments

So, lets get down to it. Lets talk about the 84 unit Shadowood Apartment property that you requested information on. The information will reveal how YOU are going to get a Guaranteed Profit! Why? A motivated seller AND a great property! You see, the current owner of this property is only the second owner of the property. Heck, he has had it almost 25 years. Now, as you can imagine, his personal life and retirement are starting to become very important to him. He also wants to travel, vacation, see friends, grandkids, help with charitable causes, etc.

So, what's holding him back? What is keeping him from enjoying his retirement to the fullest? —

Its The Apartments!

Admittedly, he is not tied down to the property, but, at his age its always there. Needing attention, supervision, etc. So much so that he thinks it is keeping him from all "later in life activities" he really wants to do. So, because he feels that he is missing out—he is motivated to move the property. He has no problem in helping the buyer MAKE MONEY WHEN YOU BUY!

Exhibit #1B Registration Form

1

VIP Action Shadowood LLC Kit Registration Form

Say "YES" Now and Reserve Your Spot By Receiving Shadowood Apartments LLC Kit That Details <u>ALL</u> Parts Of The Transaction AND How You Can Get In On IT!

Please check all that apply: (Remember, there is no obligation at this point but please be sincerely interested in this to get the LLC Kit)

☐ **I am basically IN on the Shadowood Apartments.** Enclosed is my credit card info for $500 to hold my spot as one of the first participants in this apartment buisness venture. By sending this I am guaranteeing a position to be IN the group. I understand that, if after I receive the Shadowood LLC Kit I do not have an interest I can then decline and there will be no charge against my card.

☐ I am not interested in this deal for my own reasons but please keep me posted on others like it.

☐ **I am basically IN on the Shadowood Apartments.** Enclosed is a check for $500 to hold my spot as one of the first participants in this apartment buisness venture. By sending you this $500 check I am guaranteeing a position to be IN the group. I understand that, if after I receive the Shadowood LLC Kit I do not have an interest I can then decline and receive my check back uncashed.

Name _____

Mailing Address _____

Phone (in case I have questions) _____

Credit Card # _____ Expires_____

Fax this form to #319-861-5659

Or send to:
    Darin Garman, CCIM
    116 3rd St. SE
    Cedar Rapids Iowa 52401

Part 2

The Kennedy System

Synonyms for System: methodology, process, procedure, approach, practice, framework, modus operandi, regimen, formula, routine. Writing copy that sells is *not* a creative act so much as it is mechanical **process**, adhering to **formulas**, and assembling essential component parts within a reliable **framework**.

Chapter 1

The Clay with Which to Mold

The first three steps are about getting the clay onto the worktable where we will then mold and make our masterpieces. The idea of writing a sales letter is actually something of a false idea. It suggests sitting down with a pristine, blank sheet of paper and conjuring words. In actuality, a truer description is *assembling* a sales letter. To do that, we need some things to assemble.

STEP 1: Get "Into" the Customer

An old adage says that you can't understand someone until you've walked a mile in his shoes.

It's a good adage. We entrepreneurs, for instance, would be much better off if each of our elected representatives had to spend a couple of weeks every year running a small business, struggling to meet a payroll, and filling out a slew of government forms. The people trying to work their way out of the slums would be much better off if each of our elected officials had to go live with them for a week or two every year. And our farmers would get some of their problems solved if each of those same officials had to spend a week every year working on a farm. A number of well-run companies require their top executives to take customer complaint calls periodically, open and read mail from customers, even get out into the stores and deal with customers face to face.

MORE
small businesses
are using direct mail
to attract new clients,
customers, or patients—
up to 18 percent year to year
(2010 from 2009).
(Source: 2010 U.S. Small Business Survey
reported in delivermagazine.com)

The goal is *understanding*. To persuade someone, to motivate someone, to sell someone, you really need to understand that person.

How easy is it to miss? I wrote a TV infomercial script (essentially, a sales letter that comes to life) selling a home-mortgage-related product. The script called for the spokesperson to walk into a living room, saying, "Here, in a typical American home . . ." The producer filmed this line with the spokesperson stepping into a white-carpeted room with a grand piano as its centerpiece! Out of touch, out of touch! Admittedly, most marketers are never that far out of touch with their customers or prospects, but make a mental note: the more in touch you are, the more probable your success. In my Copywriting Mastery Seminar (which hundreds of people paid $2,000.00 to attend), I provide a special checklist of smart questions to ask about your customers and prospects. (My "Copywriting Seminar in a Box" and other resources for copywriters can be found at *www.dankennedy.com*.) That check-list is reprinted here, as a very valuable "bonus" with this book.

My "10 Smart Market Diagnosis and Profiling Questions"

1. **What keeps them awake at night**, indigestion boiling up their esophagus, eyes open, staring at the ceiling?
2. What are they **afraid** of?
3. What are they **angry** about? Who are they angry at?
4. What are their top three daily **frustrations**?
5. What **trends** are occurring and will occur in their businesses or lives?
6. What do they secretly, ardently **desire** most?
7. Is there a built-in **bias** to the way they make decisions? (Example: engineers = exceptionally analytical)
8. Do they have their own **language**?
9. Who else is selling something **similar** to their product, and how?
10. Who else has tried selling them something similar, and how has that effort **failed**?

So, Step 1 in our system is to analyze thoroughly, understand, and connect with the customer.

In some cases, you may have a lot of demographic and statistical data about your customers or prospects available from your own records or from the vendors of the mailing lists you are using. You might (and probably should) know the ages, incomes, hobbies, and political affiliations of the people you're writing to—even what magazines they read regularly. Hopefully, you can even get beyond this data and gain a "feeling" for these people. If you have none of this, if you have nothing but zip codes, I'd suggest getting into your car and driving slowly, several times, on different days, through the neighborhood with one of those zip codes, to try to get a feel for those people. Or, if you're marketing to businesspeople, attend their meetings, read their trade journals.

I've spent thirty years working with the visualization techniques developed by Dr. Maxwell Maltz, author of the 30-million-copy bestseller *Psycho-Cybernetics*, and I use those techniques—like "Theater in Your Mind"—to visualize my letter's recipients as living, breathing, thinking, feeling, walking, talking human beings. I visualize their day's experience. How did it start out? What did they do when they first arrived at the office? Do they get their mail presorted? Opened? From an "in" basket? Hand-delivered? When do they get it? Where will they stand or sit when going through it? At that time, what else are they thinking about? Preoccupied with? What do they worry about, complain about, secretly wish for, enjoy? Through this stretch of my own imagination, I try to become one with the recipients of my letter, so I can anticipate their thoughts and reactions. If you don't have enough information and experience to do this, you must get it! I try to accept assignments to write sales letters only to types of prospects I know well. But given an assignment aimed at people I didn't understand, I'd go get that understanding.

Over the years, I've written hundreds of sales letters to real-estate agents. My clients have included the best-known sales trainers, seminar speakers, and marketing advisors to the real-estate profession. I am not and have never been in the real-estate business. When I first had to write a series of letters to real-estate agents, I knew nothing about their business. What did I do? I went to the public library and read several years' back issues of the trade journals that real-estate agents subscribe to and read. One of the largest real-estate companies had its convention in my city, so I went and hung out in the hotel lobby and bars and eavesdropped on conversations. I took a real-estate agent to lunch and pumped him for information. I got myself to the point where I could visualize myself as a real-estate agent and speak the language of a real-estate agent.

Once you've begun that process of identification, you'll be in a good position to determine what the recipient of your letter wants. Write these items down in order of priority.

What Is Most Important to Your Reader?

There is a classic sales legend about the hotshot salesman pitching a new home-heating system to a little old lady. He told her everything there was to tell about BTUs, construction, warranties, service, and so on. When he finally shut up, she said, "I have just one question—will this thing keep a little old lady warm?"

The mistake is even easier to make in crafting a sales letter, because there's no possibility of corrective feedback from customers during the presentation. That's why **you must determine accurately, in advance, what their priorities are. And you must address their priorities, not yours.**

I was once asked to write a corporate fundraising letter for the Arthritis Foundation's annual telethon. In examining sample letters other nonprofit organizations sent to corporate donors, I noticed that they all had the same failing in common: they talked at great length about their own priorities—what they needed the money for, how it would be used, etc.—but they hardly addressed the donor's priorities at all. So I visualized myself as the business owner or executive being banged at by all these worthy charities' pleas and asked myself, "If I were to give, what would be important to me?" I came up with this list:

1. What benefit to me or my company justifies the cost?
2. Who else had picked this drive to contribute to? (How can I validate my judgment?)
3. How would I get the money to give? (What budget would it come out of? What other expense would have to be reduced to afford this new one?)

With that list in mind, I wrote the letter reproduced on the following pages, Exhibit #2. It garnered a response of only half of 1 percent, but the responses were from important new donors—one of whom contributed a large sum. This one new donor's contribution covered about half of all the costs of the local telethon that year. Perhaps most important, every expert associated with this project believed that such a letter would not work at all. Their previous experiences told them so. And in terms of return on investment, it was the most successful fundraising effort ever mounted by this local chapter. So why did this letter work where others had failed? Because it directly addressed the interests of the recipient, not the sender!

Fundraising Facts

Direct mail is responsible for
78 percent of all donations received . . .
compared to 9 percent via the Internet.
89 percent of new donors are
acquired via direct mail.

*(Source: National Fundraising Performance Survey,
including data from 38 million donors, $2 billion
in revenue, and seventy-nine of the largest
nonprofit organizations in the world)*

Get a fix on the prospect/customer/client and on his or her desires; failing to do so will undermine all your other efforts.

How an Outsider Becomes an Insider

Here's a letter I got from my Platinum Member, Jerry Jones, president of a direct marketing and coaching company providing services to dentists nationwide:

"Back in 1997, after about two months of owning this business, I read the '10 Smart Questions' in this chapter. The list exposed my biggest handicap in marketing to dentists: not being one of them. Because I'm not the customer in my niche, I have had to work hard at understanding what motivates them, keeps them awake at night, what the current desirable carrot is to them. Here are six things I do to stay in that frame of mind. And I'm apparently managing to do it, because I am frequently accused of being a dentist!

1. I read *every* industry publication *every* month.
2. I visit websites that host discussion forums for dentists.
3. I subscribe to e-mail groups where only dentists communicate back and forth.
4. I attend industry functions, conventions, seminars, and trade shows.

5. I 'play prospect' with other product and service providers to dentists.
6. I routinely 'mastermind' with dentists and with other marketers and vendors who provide services to the profession.

I think this is so important that I even invested in three dental practices to get more firsthand understanding and to have laboratories to test my new strategies, ideas, direct-mail campaigns, and products."

Exhibit #2

_____ Director of Marketing

Dear _____:

Special, **highly effective TV exposure** at half the ordinary cost, even a smaller fraction of the ordinary cost—even free! Yes, it is possible.

Our annual **ARTHRITIS FOUNDATION TELETHON** has moved to CHANNEL 10 (Phoenix' CBS affiliate), and we are offering an expanded, more flexible, more creative range of Sponsor Opportunities to businesses of all sizes in the valley.

Many corporate sponsors last year actually participated spending little or no money—the funds were raised through fundraising events or promotions involving their employees or customers. For example, one major corporation used several Employee Promotions, and raised over $50,000.00. A small company used a Bowl-A-Thon with their employees, employees' family members, and friends, and raised $5,000.00. Both received excellent exposure on the Telethon. **AND THIS YEAR, THE OPPORTUNITIES ARE EVEN GREATER.**

There are many different Sponsor Programs available including several that give you a competition-free exclusive position. Sponsors are needed for each hour for the phone banks; for the Interview Area, where guests are interviewed by celebrity hosts; for table banners; and much more. There are even a few 1 and 2 minute Video Presentation Opportunities (company exposure) available. In all cases, representatives of your firm come on the show for you, your people, and your products. We will also assist you every step of the way with your employee fundraising event or other promotion, to raise the funds for your sponsorship. There really is no good reason not to participate.

As a sponsor, you'll be showing your concern for the community, in connection with a situation that, at one time or another, will affect over 35% of all families! Arthritis is one of the most common, frustrating, debilitating diseases. It is understandably of great concern to a great many people. Also, the Arthritis Foundation has an excellent track record in terms of appropriate use of funds for research and education (rather than organizational overhead). We believe that real cures for arthritis are just around the corner; you can help get us there!

With our Telethon on Channel 10, we will benefit from their superior production capability, involvement of their popular celebrities, and advance promotional opportunities. Our Telethon will be on for several hours immediately before and again immediately after an NBA Basketball Game, which we believe will increase our viewership. And, of course, we're mixing our live, local show with a "feed" from the National Telethon, featuring major Hollywood entertainers. Everything points to our highest, most responsive viewership ever!

You'll be in good company, too, with local and national sponsors like: **Thrifty, Sears, Allstate, Greyhound, Prudential, and Procter & Gamble.**

To summarize, you have an opportunity to . . .

1. Help a good, worthy cause
2. Gain valuable TV exposure and publicity
3. Get all the benefits with little or no money out of your present budget—we'll work with your employees to raise the funds!
4. Possibly have exclusive position, if you act quickly
5. Have complete, step-by-step assistance from our staff

Why not give me a call; let's arrange a meeting where I can personally explain the different "standard opportunities" available and then "brainstorm" with you about the best way for your business to participate. There's no obligation, of course, and certainly no pressure, but, together, we just may figure out the perfect situation for your business.

Thank you for you consideration,

Joel L. Beck
Telethon Chairman for the Arthritis Foundation

JLB/va

Letter reprinted with permission of Dan Kennedy (writer) and Joel Beck, former telethon chairman, Arizona.

Jerry's an extremely astute marketer who has enjoyed enormous success doing something that is generally difficult to do; becoming a respected, sought-after coach, consultant, and guru to a profession he's never been a part of. It's far more common for the guru to have come up through the same industry, to have been where his students and clients are.

Acquiring a deep understanding of the target customer should not be short-changed—by anyone writing sales copy, at any time, for any purpose.

As I was writing this edition of this book, I was writing copy for a long-time client, the Guthy-Renker Corporation, for their hugely successful Proactiv® brand of acne products. There are three different people to talk to about this—the teen sufferer, the teen's mom, and playing the odds, the adult female sufferer. This had me reading past and current issues of nearly a hundred magazines, including all the teen and preteen magazines, all the mom magazines, and all the women's magazines, having copious online research done for me, doing "conversational research" directly with people in all three groups, and even hiring a dozen freelance readers—teens, parents of teens, and young women—to critique my copy. Also, as I was writing this edition of this book, I began work on copy aimed at highly successful, professional financial and investment advisors, financial planners, and top-performing life insurance and annuities agents, which required a similar investment of time and energy in crawling inside their psyche, tribal language, daily experiences. Freelance writers worth their salt know they must do this sort of thing, and do. **The danger for the business owner writing copy for himself and for his own business is *ingrained assumption*—** encouraging shortcutting or altogether neglecting this step. The only sure way to keep your own accumulated but untested opinions and beliefs about your customers from sabotaging your sales letters is to start anew, from scratch, and to engage in getting to know the customers just as if you were arriving to write for them for the first time, with no foreknowledge.

ADVANCED SALES COPY STRATEGY #1

One of American History's Most Unusual Copywriters' Most Prized Strategies Lives in Every Top Copywriter's Toolbox

Here's an advanced thinking strategy designed to get you into the customer's frame of mind before you write that dates to the 1930s.

Its "inventor" was, in his life, an unordained minister and author of several religious/spiritual books, including *The Secret of the Ages*, and a spectacularly successful advertising copywriter, selling everything from raincoats to magazines by mail order in the 1930s and 1940s. His name: Robert Collier. He is widely credited for the Collier Principle: "Always enter the conversation already occurring in the customer's mind."

The news/opinion show on MSNBC hosted by Keith Olberman has, in its opening, this line: "What will you be talking about tomorrow?" This is a very powerful question to ask about your customers, rephrased as "What will your customers be thinking about and talking about the day they receive or see your sales copy?"

Collier understood and preached this swim-with-current-rather-than-against strategy. Do not arrive as an interruption or disruption, attempting to divert your reader's attention from the object it is focused on, fighting to interest him in something different from what he is already, at this moment, interested in. Instead, align yourself with the subjects already possessing his attention, the matters already garnering his interest, the self-talk conversation already occurring in his mind, and the conversations he is already having around the water-cooler at work or at the kitchen table at home with peers, friends, and family.

About this, Collier wrote: "Study your reader first—your product second. . . . The reader of your letter wants certain things and the desire for them is, consciously or unconsciously, the dominant idea in his mind all the time. He is also engaged by the news or events or public conversations of the day. Put yourself in his place. If you were deep in discussion with a friend over some matter and a stranger came up and said: 'Mister, I have a fine coat I want to sell you!'—what would you do? The same thing happens when you approach a man by mail. He is in discussion with himself. If you just butt in, will you be welcome? How would you do it if approaching him and his friend in person? You'd listen and get the trend of the conversation. Then, when you chimed in, it would be with a remark on a related subject. Then you could gradually bring the talk around logically to the point you wanted to discuss. Study your reader. Know what interests him. Listen to the conversation he is already having with himself. Enter where he already is."

There are some obvious, perennially occurring attention dominators, such as seasons and holidays, and linking to these—regardless of whether your business naturally links or not—can be extremely helpful. You need not be a florist, jeweler, or restaurant to utilize Valentine's Day, for example. Beyond that, and deeper than that, every customer group has some shared item on their minds. Know it. Start your conversation with them with it. And be sure to take advantage of one of the great advantages of today's online media, including e-mail, blogs, and social media sites—being day to day, even hour by hour, timely. You can link a marketing message to world or local, financial, or cultural news of the moment—and you should.

STEP 2: Get "Into" the Offer

Just as you try to crawl inside the letter recipient's mind and heart, you want to crawl around in your product or service, too

If you're writing a letter to promote a product, get the product, use it as the consumer would, play with it, test it, take it apart and put it back together, even demonstrate it to others as a salesperson would. If you're writing a letter to promote a service, use it yourself if possible. Go talk to those who do use it. Talk to people who use a competitive service. If you're writing a letter to promote a special offer, do everything possible to analyze that offer. Try it out on people. Find out if they understand it, if they're intrigued by it.

Build a List of Product/Offer Features and Benefits

I like to put each item on separate 3-by-5-inch cards so I can shuffle them after I've written them all out and sort them according to importance. This works better for me than a list on a sheet of paper. Sometimes I tack the cards up in a vertical row on a bulletin board in my office so it's easy for me to keep looking at them as I write. This is essentially a brainstorming exercise. You can do it alone, aided by product literature. Or you can do it with a group of participants. Either way, the idea is to list every possible feature and benefit, then organize them by importance.

Note that I said "features and benefits." It's amazing how easily people fall into talking about the features of their product or service, instead of the benefits it provides. I find myself constantly reminding our clients: **"People do not buy things for what they are; they buy things for what they do."**

Now, here is an advanced copywriting secret, courtesy of my friend Ted Nicholas: the use of **"the *hidden* benefit."** Ted has personally sold over $200 million worth of how-to books via direct-response ads in magazines and newspapers and via sales letters, and retired relatively young to Switzerland on the proceeds, so he knows a thing or two about salesmanship-in-print. Ted often looks for what he calls the hidden benefit to emphasize. This means it's not the obvious benefit—not the first benefit you think of—yet one that is of profound importance to your customer.

I'll give you an actual example. Pamela Yellen, the CEO of the Prospecting & Marketing Institute, based in Santa Fe, New Mexico, and I were conducting a multiday seminar for her clients—corporate executives and general agents from life insurance companies—about new methods of recruiting agents. Even though the attendees had paid a very high per-person fee to be there, most had traveled great distances, and the subject was of critical importance to them, we both noticed that on breaks, what most of them were talking about was where they were going to go play golf that evening when the seminar let out, the next morning before it started, or the day afterward. Both Pamela and I made note of how important it was to these clients of hers to get out on the golf course.

This led to one of the most unusual ads Pamela has ever written and run in her own industry's trade journals, with the headline: "Puts Recruiting on Autopilot So You Can Go Play Golf!" The entire ad is reproduced on the following page, Exhibit #3. As you'll see, it sold the system we devised for insurance agent recruiting, but it did so circuitously, by emphasizing the hidden benefit: you'll get the job done with less time invested, so you can spend more time on the golf course.

Exhibit #3 Golf Advertisement

Are you **tired** of **struggling** with recruiting? **Unexcited** about endlessly pumping everyone you know for names?
Burned-out from chasing after candidates day after day?
FREE report reveals how revolutionary Magnetic Recruiting System:

"Puts Recruiting On Auto-Pilot So You Can Go Play Golf!"

Exciting, new, but already proven system causes qualified, enthusiastic candidates to literally chase you down!

"I ran a small classified ad once in a Sunday paper and a series of inexpensive radio spots over the course of a week, according to the formula I learned from **Magnetic Recruiting**, and got 11 appointments from it. Every one of those people called me. 10 were excellent quality, not one single person was a no-show and I found three people worth hiring in the bunch! **Magnetic Recruiting** definitely causes a lot of excitement in the agency, gets the whole office involved, creates a lot of activity and attracts good, solid quality candidates."
—George K., PA

"The candidates I see through Magnetic Recruiting are the types of candidates I really want to work with and the ones that stick. The system is consistent, predictable and attracts high quality candidates. It allows me to determine which river I'm going to pan gold from, as opposed to the hit-and-miss method we've been using in this industry, and how many gold nuggets are going to come out the other end. Magnetic Recruiting is a better way to pan for gold. Once it's set up in your agency, it's automatic."—Victor L. BC, Canada

"**Magnetic Recruiting** gets me an additional 18 to 22 booked appointments every month with some of the most exceptional candidates I've ever seen—and every one of them called ME! I'm seeing highly successful corporate executives and managers, bankers, attorneys and CPAs, successful sales professionals in other fields and business owners all the time now. Magnetic Recruiting saves me an inordinate amount of time, puts the entire process on auto-pilot and allows me to spend time on the right things. The candidates who come in to talk to me already know they're going to be selling insurance and financial services, and yet they usually try to convince me that they're the right person for the job!"—Tim M., OH

"**Magnetic Recruiting** maximizes recruiting efficiency by minimizing interviews with poor candidates. Eliminates the excuse of not having recruits to talk to."—Bob K., NC

"**Magnetic Recruiting** attracts some of the highest caliber candidates from cold sources I've ever seen. I routinely have executives in downsizing companies and others earning $100–$200,000 a year coming in to see me. For the first time I have people from cold sources seeking me out trying to convince me they're the one instead of me trying to sell them on the virtues of our career. It saves me a half day of work every week and my secretary handles it all. All I do now is accept candidates' calls and show up for the interview."—Saul C., NY

Would you like to have a predictable flow of interested, high-caliber candidates calling YOU and working hard to convince you to accept them? Dream candidates who already know what your opportunity is all about?

If you'd like to have complete control over your recruiting process, regardless of the economy or any other market condition and put an end to the endless grunt work you've become resigned to, please keep reading.

Getting Candidates to Call YOU Is Easy...If You Know the Best Kept Marketing Secret!

Maybe you too have found that recruiting is getting tougher. You have to talk to a lot more people than ever before. Maybe, it's been awhile since recruiting was actually fun. Or, you may be in that happy minority having a great recruiting year. But you're still not where you want to be. Perhaps you're sick of pumping your agents and nominators for names. Chasing after people who aren't interested in hearing your story. Seminars that hardly seem worth the bother.

You see, success at getting plenty of qualified candidates has a lot more to do with understanding the real secrets of direct-response marketing...and little to do with chasing after prospects. Whether this is your first year in management, or you're a thirty year veteran, you will love to never again talk to anyone unless they have CALLED YOU!

Your Competition is Using These Magnetic Recruiting Techniques to Steal Your Best Prospects...With a Story Half as Good as Yours!

The business opportunity, franchise and distributorship industries are currently booming like never before. There are today far more people looking for you, than there are you looking for them!

So why is recruiting down? The biggest obstacle you face is marketing incest. Everyone goes to the same meetings, listens to the same speakers, reads the same publications. Just like when people inbreed, it doesn't take very long before everyone gets stupid. Breakthroughs come from going "outside the box" and bringing new, proven, translated systems back in. Keep doing what you've always done and you can be sure as shootin' you'll never get anything different than what you've already got.

Now There's a New, **100% Measurable Replacement For Old-Fashioned Recruiting Grunt Work!**

Imagine how your life would be different if you only talked to candidates who CALLED YOU, and were really interested in your opportunity! Do you think you'd feel more successful if you didn't need to constantly badger everyone for names? This is no pipe dream.

FREE Report Tells All!

You can be the greatest manager in the world—but that won't do you a bit of good if you can't attract enough of the right people. So, if you are ready to discover the astonishing secrets of getting qualified candidates to call you, CALL NOW!

1-800-856- (US and Canada), 24-hours-a-day for FREE recorded message and to get your FREE Report!

Or, write "Recruiting" on your business card and fax to

STEP 3: Create a Damaging Admission and Address Flaws Openly

This may seem strange to you at first, but identifying the flaws in your product, service, or offer is a big step forward toward making the sale.

By acknowledging the flaws, you force yourself to address your letter recipient's questions, objections, and concerns. You also enhance your credibility.

Figure Out Why They Won't Respond

People are damned contrary creatures! You present them with a perfectly good offer and they still don't respond—why not? I think it was Yogi Berra who said something along the lines of, "When people don't want to come to the ballpark, there ain't nothing that can keep 'em from not coming." Well, there are lots of reasons not to come to the ballpark. Again, I like to use 3-by-5-inch cards and put a reason for not responding on each card. I try to think of every possible objection, concern, fear, doubt, and excuse someone might use to keep from responding.

I talked with a doctor about a particular product being marketed through the mail by a company competitive with my own. The doctor told me that he had received at least a dozen sales letters from that company, had read them, and was interested in the product; I knew he had the financial ability to buy. So why hadn't he? He told me that he felt the offer was too good to be true, and that made him skeptical about everything said about the product. If the marketer had anticipated that reaction and answered it somewhere in his letter, he would certainly have increased the response to his mailings.

Honestly Assess the Disadvantages of Your Offer and Face Them

Every product, service, and offer has some unattractive points. Nothing's perfect, and everybody knows that. By admitting and openly discussing the drawbacks to your offer, your "credibility stock" goes way up on most of your letter recipients' charts. This is called "damaging admission copy." Consider this example from a sales letter sent to area residents by a small Italian restaurant:

> If you want waiters in tuxedos with white linen cloths over their arms, menus with unpronounceable words all over them, and high-priced wines served in silver ice buckets when you go out for Italian food, our little restaurant is not the place to come. But if you mostly want good, solid, home-cooked pasta with tasty sauces made with real vegetables and spices by a real Italian Mama and will trade white linen for red-and-white checked plastic tablecloths, you'll like our place just fine. If you're okay with a choice of just two wines, red or white, we'll give you as much of it as you want, from our famous bottomless wine bottle—free with your dinner.

This restaurant owner took competitive disadvantages and turned them into a good, solid, "fun" selling story.

This gives you copywriting fodder from an unusual source— the flaws and disadvantages of your product, service, business, or proposition. Instead of looking at them as problems and obstacles to a sale, look at them as building blocks in a believable, interesting, and persuasive message.

Chapter 2

Salmon Swimming Upstream

Sales letters face hazards en route to readership. From the very beginning of assembling your sales letter, you need to have formulated the way you will armor your letter to confront and conquer its enemies and hazards, as it makes its way from you to the hands and eyes of the person you hope will read it. This has to be considered early, because what is on the outside of its envelope or other exterior has to influence what's inside, and what's inside has to influence what's outside. Not that I'd recommend it in most cases anyway, but you can't use a giant, hot-pink, metallic envelope with the word *Sex* on it and inside have a dull letter on law firm letterhead warning of estate law changes that need to be addressed in the reader's will. The next two steps have to do with the outside of whatever package delivers your sales letter. . . .

STEP 4: Get Your Sales Letter Delivered

Early in the process of putting together your sales letter, you need to think about getting the finished letter into the hands of people who can respond.

There are two delivery dangers to consider:

First, the U.S. Postal Service itself. There's some ebb and flow to this, but both the media as watchdog and USPS itself have often caught and exposed dramatic incidents of deliberate nondelivery, such as dumpsters or even entire barns full of accumulated, undelivered mail, as well as a low-grade, continuous cancer of some percentage of all mail never arriving at its intended destinations, day to day, everyday. There are many reasons for this, many of which are beyond your influence. But one that is within your control is the appearance of the outside of the envelope. If it screams "junk mail," it tempts weary sorters and carriers to chuck it without fear of repercussion. If it appears to be important or desired or bought and paid for, so that somebody not receiving it as expected might squawk, it is less likely to be delivered to the dumpster behind the doughnut shop. This is one of the premises behind outer envelopes designed to fool or at least influence the postal carriers, such as good, fake "Express Delivery" envelope faces or official-looking or personal-looking faces.

Second, the gatekeepers—that is, the people you have to rely on to get your letters into the hands of the intended recipient. In B2B, there may be one, there may be several, standing—and sorting—between your epistle and its intended reader. Even someone in the letter recipient's office or own home could be an obstacle, tossing the letter before the intended recipient even sees it.

With these challenges to getting your prose delivered to the correct person in mind, following are some delivery options to weigh and consider.

Means of Delivery

Mail is certainly not the only choice. I've had clients send tens of thousands of FedEx envelopes, boxes and tubes by UPS, and packages hand-delivered by messenger services. The value of the response governs what can be spent, of course, but sometimes the most expensive option provides such superior results that it is the true bargain. Of all of these, a FedEx envelope or package remains the thing least likely to be waylaid or delayed and least likely to be delayed or discarded by gatekeepers.

With mail, you choose class of delivery, and *class* is a good word for it. Bulk mail that is clearly bulk mail has two profound disadvantages: slowness and uncertainty of timely delivery or even delivery at all, as the deliberate nondelivery problem is at its worst with bulk, and the perception by carriers and recipients that it is unimportant or "junk." Bulk, however, has at the advantage that it is the lowest cost available to most mailers, although there are nonprofit rates and periodical publisher rates. In most situations, I advocate using first-class mail if you can possibly adjust the economics of your business to allow for it. The USPS isn't making this any easier, with its too-frequent, somewhat desperate rate increases, but I remain a die-hard holdout for first class.

Live Stamps Versus Meter Indices

Again, postal workers are least likely to dispose of mail they believe recipients are expecting, and gatekeepers are least likely to trash mail that appears to be individually prepared and sent. Meter imprints or postage imprints bought online and downloaded from your own computer scream "mass mail," not correspondence. For this reason, the savviest, most successful direct-mail marketers continue to affix actual postage stamps to their envelopes, and so should you.

Labels, Ink-Jet, Typewriter, Faux Hand-Addressed, or Real Hand-Addressed Envelopes

A gummed white label is a dead giveaway, and if you insist on using them, or for some weird reason, must use them, you might as well use an interesting or colorful label, and you might as well use bulk mail if you like. Ink-jet addressing keeps getting better and better, and can mimic typewriters or handwriting quite effectively, although still imperfectly. And bad fake handwriting is just as bad as the mass-produced gummed label. Envelopes actually addressed by hand often outperform all others in controlled split-tests. For a number of years I had an interest in a business mailing as many as 25,000 hand-addressed envelopes every week, prepared by a small army of stay-at-home moms paid by the piece, and despite all the available technology, were I in a business doing "cold" direct mail to new prospects today, I'd still do exactly the same thing.

The Sneak-Up Approach

A plain white envelope with no business name, only an address with no name or a person's name as the return address; no teaser copy; individual or ink-jet addressing; and a live stamp—all this makes your mailing look like a letter, not advertising or junk mail. It then stands the highest possible chance of completed delivery. Given that design and first-class postage, I'd give it a 98 percent chance of getting there and getting opened.

Intimidating Imprints

"Audited Delivery . . . Verified Delivery . . . The Information You Requested Is Enclosed . . . Important Documents Enclosed . . . ." Imprints or affixed gold seals with this kind of wording seem to work well. Exhibit #4 is one I received back in 1985. This shows you how evergreen this strategy is, because the strategy hasn't changed, and these kinds of "official-looking labels" are frequently used in political, fundraising, and business-to-business mailings to increase likelihood of delivery by the postal folks and by company mailroom clerks, secretaries, and other gatekeepers.

I suggest that you begin saving the envelopes from your own incoming mail and sorting them by how they are addressed. Pay closer attention to the ones that pass the "smell test" for important or personal—those that gatekeepers are less likely to discard and that interest you and motivate you to open them—versus mass or junk mail—those that are easily discarded and that would be easier for postal workers or gatekeepers to fearlessly discard.

Exhibit #4 Intimidating Imprints

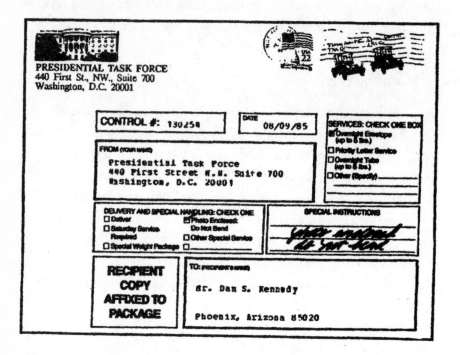

STEP 5: Get Your Sales Letter Looked At

Let's optimistically assume that the lion's share of your mail survives the vagaries of postal delivery and moves through gatekeepers to the stack on the desk or kitchen counter of its intended recipient.

Just about everybody throws out some mail unopened. Letters that do get opened and looked at have only a quick heartbeat to survive the sort, avoid the wastebasket, and earn the attention and interest of the recipient.

The best and most succinct advice I ever got on this subject is from a true direct-marketing genius, the late Gary Halbert. Gary said, **"Pic-**

ture the person you've sent your sales letter to with a stack of mail in his hands, sorting through that stack, standing next to a wastebasket."

You might write that up as a sign and post it on your wall:

America sorts its mail standing over a wastebasket.

---

2 OUT of 3
consumers say
they prefer
print catalogs
to online catalogs.
(Source: PitneyBowes Research)

Wow! That is an insight worth a great deal of money. Think of it this way: People prejudge their mail, just as they do other people, places, books, and so on. That may be unfair or unreasonable, but it really happens.

Even I, a mail junkie, student, and collector, have days and sometimes weeks when I am just too busy to open and look at every piece of mail that crosses my various desks. I receive mail at my office and personal mail at two different private mail services in my two home cities. During busy times, when I receive these boxes of mail, I stand right next to the wastebasket. The mail from my office has been presorted for me, divided into Urgent, Personal, A-pile Business, Other, Catalogs and Magazines. The other mail has not been presorted. So, if I'm really time-pressed, I create a new A-pile, a B-pile that will wait, but I also ruthlessly discard as much as I can, unopened, unread.

Let me give you an example of how big an impact this can have. I have had and have a number of clients who mail extensively to chiropractors, dentists, cosmetic surgeons, and medical doctors, and, over the years, I've tried every kind of envelope look you can imagine. By far, the mailings that pull best are sent in "plain Jane" envelopes without a company name on them, but, instead, a doctor's name and return address. Staff do not screen these envelopes. The doctor opens them. The response to these mailings versus the same letters sent in different, more "honest" envelopes is sometimes as much as 300 percent higher!

Mailing to consumers at their homes carries a different set of problems. First of all, it is my admittedly informal observation that in most households most of the mail is sorted and handled by the woman, not the man. And today's extraordinarily busy working woman is ruthless in handling this mail. Much of it hits the trash without seeing the light of day.

So, how do *you* get *your* sales letter opened? The same strategies I just described for fooling postal employees and gatekeepers also serve to motivate recipients to open the envelope. If you are going to use a devious strategy, the most important thing to remember is that you must quickly fulfill the envelope's promise inside. For example, when we mail with a doctor's name as our return address, we enclose a little scratchpad-size "lift letter" from that doctor that says: "The information presented here has been of immense value to me and I thought it might interest you, also. The Publisher asked me to let you know how much I've gained from his service and I was glad to do so. You'll do yourself a favor by reading everything enclosed. Sincerely . . ." Similarly, if your envelope says "Personal" outside, there had better be something personal inside. Unfulfilled envelope promises destroy the credibility of everything enclosed and everything you have to say. Fulfilled envelope promises work to enhance your credibility.

The Opposite of Sneak-Up

Despite everything said in this chapter and the preceding chapter, the overwhelming majority of direct mail *does* clearly identify itself as a salesperson arriving, with business identity, logo, and "teaser copy." My own tendency is to use the techniques discussed previously in these chapters when reaching out to new prospects for the first time, but to switch to using the outside of the envelope to get the reader excited and curious about what's inside when mailing to established customers who recognize and respect the sender. **My rule is: never be half-pregnant.** If you are going to reveal that you are sending business mail or sales material via a company name, meter imprint, or even one line of "teaser copy," like "Inside: 10 Ways to Cut Your Ad Budget By 70 Percent but Sell More!" then you might as well use the entire envelope as a billboard and sell, sell, sell!

A good example is this envelope created for a client of mine, Rory Fatt, for a mailing about one of his seminars for restaurant owners. As you can see in Exhibit #5, the whole face of the envelope is a billboard. There's teaser copy, a photo of a car being given away—and note the personalization. Each recipient's name appears on the license plate of the car!

Exhibit #5 Envelope Example

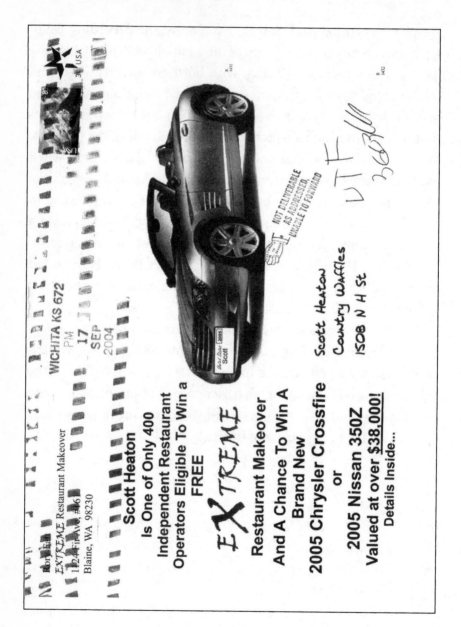

Because few restaurant owners have aggressive gatekeepers between them and their mail, and because Rory was mailing to clients he already has a relationship with, I advised this approach, and it was very successful. There is still risk of postal nondelivery, but there is high probability of the recipient being motivated to open it when it is received. If this was being sent instead to corporate executives with a gatekeeper in the way, I might have put this envelope inside a simple kraft envelope, personally addressed, only with Rory's name in the return address corner, and it might be sent via FedEx or Priority Mail, in their outer envelopes.

As you can see, in each instance, I invest a great deal of thought to getting the mail delivered and delivered to the targeted decision-maker—and you should too!

The Power of Personalization

One of the latest discoveries that many of my clients are using is what I call a "hybrid envelope." It crossbreeds personalization with teaser copy. A leader in developing and using this approach is Bill Glazer. Shown here, Exhibits #6 and #7, is the front and back of a 9-by-2-inch envelope sent to cold prospects, in this case furniture store owners. The front is a window envelope with a personalized sales letter showing through. The city and state and the individual's name is in the letter's headline, and you can see "Dear Rebecca" in the window as well. Yes, each one is personalized, and the technology exists to do this easily. But also note that the front of the envelope has teaser copy too (which is printed in blue ink).

Then the back is printed as a billboard, every inch covered with testimonials.

I think you'll agree, this is an unusual and powerful approach.

Exhibit #6 Glazer Envelope (front)

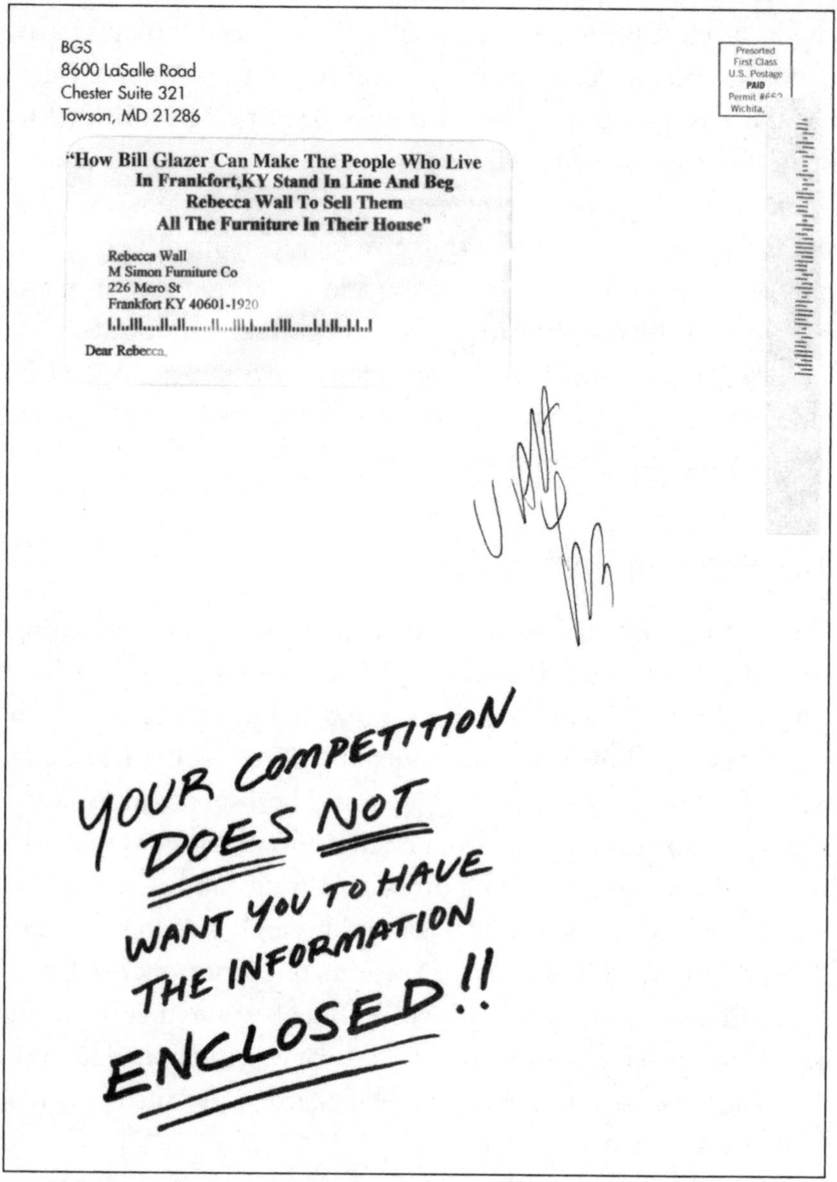
BGS
8600 LaSalle Road
Chester Suite 321
Towson, MD 21286
Presorted
First Class
U.S. Postage
PAID
Wichita,
"How Bill Glazer Can Make The People Who Live In Frankfort,KY Stand In Line And Beg Rebecca Wall To Sell Them All The Furniture In Their House"
Rebecca Wall
M Simon Furniture Co
226 Mero St
Frankfort KY 40601-1920
Dear Rebecca,
YOUR COMPETITION DOES NOT WANT YOU TO HAVE THE INFORMATION ENCLOSED!!

Exhibit #7 Glazer Envelope (back)

FIND OUT HOW THESE FURNITURE SHOP OWNERS HAVE DISCOVERED SUCCESS!!!

★ Bill,

just wanted to drop you and note to tell you that I took one of your mailings right out of your Marketing System, mailed it for my furniture store, and it was the most successful promotion we have ever held.

We have also successfully used Voice Broadcast to or customers exactly how you reach it and added a 25% increase to an existing sale that we have held before.

Finally, I want to report that we have implemented your "Customer Loyalty" program and not only do our customers love it, but it brings them back more frequently. As you can imagine, this is always a challenge in the furniture business.

Thanks for everything!

★ Every retailer needs a continuing source of new ideas, and Bill is one of the best sources I've found.
— **John W. Cole / Walker Bros.**

★ I'M A FURNITURE RETAILER. What I know about Bill Glazer's Marketing System is that he brings us fresh ideas from many different retail niches other than the "same old, same old" that I see in furniture.

Since investing in the System, I've already implemented a Frequent Buyers Program designed to bring back existing customers more often, and a Referral Program designed to get my customers to refer their friends and family members to my store.

Perhaps the biggest change in thinking for me was Bill got me to understand that it was a lot less expensive to bring back previous customers instead of wasting time and money on "expensive" ads, trying to attract new customers.
— **Ron Wessel / Love Furniture Galleries**

★ Everyone can benefit from BGS Marketing materials. The chapter on referral programs and attracting customers by new associates are worth the price of admission. And, anyone considering cable TV must see the tape for great ideas.
— **Andrew Mattor / Andrew Davis**

★ After spending many years interacting with and marketers in my business, your abilities are, for superior to all the rest. Most so-called experts create information with no experience in the real world. Your strategies go to the next level. You live and breathe every aspect of your business, and you have an amazing ability to translate your depth of knowledge into creating great events and promotions that garner high response rates from your customers.
— **Sam and Leslie Fishbein / Kacey Fine Furniture**

★ The ideas, techniques, and strategies we've gleaned from Mr. Glazer have helped us to re-design our approach to our total advertising efforts this year. Each time we follow Bill's lead, we end up with a greater focus and the results have shown in our written sales in our increase of 11.23% in the last 9 months (as compared to the same period the previous last).
— **David Kessler / Flooring Xpress**

★ After "72 years in business" we often have struggled to come up wit new promotions and events to being our customers back on a more frequent and consistent basis. The BGS Marketing System has given us a real "shot in the arm." We have now developed a formal marketing committee that meets regularly to plan store events. While many of the concepts within the BGS had been practiced at our store, this introduced many new ways to approach them. We've completely reinvented our Rewards program, and we've activated a Referral System. Thanks BGS Marketing renewing the enthusiasm in my business.
— **Daniel E. Reynolds / Stephenson's**

★ Independent business owners who do not have cookie cutter franchises are desperate for entrepreneurial direction and your counsel is the most comprehensive I have ever seen (I have 25 years experience). BGS Marketing keeps reminding us of the common sense marketing ideas we so often forget to use or, even worse, stop using because we are bored with these simple direct mail ideas or the secret possible scenarios - we are too lazy to act on them. Even if your think you're busy and running at 60 mph, Bill's advertising ideas are guaranteed to improve your marketing efforts.
— **Rob Herzog / Herzog's**

★ Have been with BGS for close to a year. The parts that apply to my store are invaluable. They truly keep us focused. Our customer response is mailings has jumped from approximately 2% to as high as 10%
— **G.A. Kourns / Kaly's Boutique**

★ The system has breathed new life into our business. The final reductions sale promotion alone has turned the "bad" months into my 3rd and 4th best months of the year. Now I have to plan off price buys just to keep up with demand! A good problem to have.
— **Tim Hare / Riverside Shop**

★ Dear Bill,
We have been with your program a little over 2 years. It takes a while to become a believer even when we know what what we are told works. Last Christmas we did a 3-page letter following your strategies with and got a 16% return on the mailing. For a small community of less than 4,000 people we were ecstatic.
— **Keith Bryan / Bryan's**

★ I received your kit in middle of our 100th anniversary sale. It was, so far, a complete flop. The old newspaper ads no longer work. I studied your material day and night, hours & hours. Then I sent out a mailing using the exact techniques you teach. *Finally customers started coming in Prepared to Buy!* Thanks. It's great!

★ Your Marketing System is great! Everything is so well prepared. The information is broken down for the busy retailer and easy to understand. Great information from all facets of marketing is funneled down that enables me to take a new approach to my business. Thanks for all you do. (Any retailer not using your Marketing System doesn't know what they are missing.)
— **Dick Lerner / Bel Air Fashion**

★ We have utilized the BGS System for sometime now...The lowest common denominator is this - If you take one idea and change it slightly to match your personal style, you will find tremendous success. This system works.
— **Jay Tollett / Collins & Williams**

★ Bill—
Thanks to you and your marketing system we are not participating in the recession!

Operating as a family business for sixty-plus years we were not accustomed to sales decreases, however, after 9-11 our sales began to decrease from 5% up (20% each month). We even had considered closing over business.

When we heard about the Bill Glazer Marketing System, we felt that this was by far the solution to our problems. We knew that we were "up against a brick wall." And at last we decided to try the system.

After reading your manuals, and listening to your tapes, we began to implement some of the strategies. We began to see our sales increase - from a 20% decrease in December to a 5% increase in March, and a 16% increase in April.

We are glad things about us we continue to implement more Bill Glazer Strategies! And mail entire at seventy-six years old! Why we haven't touched the tip of the iceberg yet! Just watch our sales grow.
— **Lloyd Stephens / Stephens of Mendenhall, Inc.**

YOU'LL FIND EVEN MORE SUCCESS STORIES INSIDE...

ADVANCED SALES COPY STRATEGY #2

Magic Words

Would you like some well-tested, time-tested, consistently effective Magic Words you can use on the outside of envelopes that will dramatically improve their getting-opened numbers? Here are choices:

PHOTO ENCLOSED: DO NOT BEND

This works because everybody likes looking at pictures, curiosity is aroused about the photos, and there's the idea of something of value as well.

HEALTH ALERT FOR RESIDENTS OF TWIN OAKS

This can be tweaked. It could be a business alert for '*x*', a financial alert for '*y*', a neighborhood alert for parents in '*z*', etc. What makes it work is the area or other customization and the word '*Alert*'.

YOUR TICKETS ENCLOSED: PLEASE OPEN IMMEDIATELY

This can be used for free seminars, at-store events (even "closed door" sales), restaurant events, fundraisers, etc.

REFUND ENCLOSED

Or: Rebate Enclosed. Works with the window envelope with a fake check showing through—and can multiply opening of that kind of envelope. Obviously, a "story" must be crafted to match.

Happy Birthday

On a birthday card-size envelope, timed for delivery the month or week of the recipient's birthday. (Resource Note: the leading expert on birthday-based mailing lists and birthday-themed mailings for new customer acquisition is Dean Killingbeck, of New Customers Now Marketing, *www.newcustomersnowmarketing.com*.)

PS: You'll notice each of the Magic-Word phrases is shown here in a different, appropriate typeface. Appearance matters. Refer to Chapter 8 for more information about this.

Chapter 3

Eyes Wide Shut

The best sales letter in the world is worthless in the hands of the willfully blind. There is a natural and understandable but unwarranted assumption undermining most sales letters: because you sent it, they'll read it. Sort of like: if you build it, they will come. Cute idea for a movie, but in the cold, cruel real world few feel obligated to come simply because somebody poured money into construction. Another movie title gives warning: *Gone in 60 Seconds*. That's what your recipients will be if you do not command their attention and literally drag them into reading. Step 6 in this chapter can give your sales letter the arms and hands it needs to grab the recipient and force him to begin reading.

STEP 6: Get Your Sales Letter Read

In person-to-person selling, there is a little formula taught almost universally: AIDA, which stands for: **A**ttention, **I**nterest, **D**esire, **A**ction. This is the orderly process of a sale. So, once you've gotten the letter recipient's attention, you must work to develop his or her interest.

From Annoying Pest to Quite Welcome Guest

One warm afternoon I was at home alone, sitting at my kitchen counter, a large iced tea in hand, talking on the telephone with an important client in another city. The doorbell rang. I ignored it. It rang relentlessly. I ignored it. Then the uninvited, unwanted pest pounded on the door. "Damn," I said to myself—but I still tried to continue my conversation. Suddenly there was someone banging on the sliding glass door behind me; at this stage it was a contest of wills and I refused to even turn around and look. Then he was back banging on the front door. I finally excused myself from the conversation and went to the door to get rid of this guy.

He was a passing motorist trying to tell me that the shrubs along my backyard wall were in flames!

Suddenly this guy was elevated in status from annoying pest to welcome guest! Clearly, he was on my side: "Get the hose going—I'll call the fire department!" Together we kept the burning shrubbery from setting my whole house on fire.

How did he go from pest to welcome guest so quickly? Because he had something to tell me that I instantly recognized as of urgent importance and of great value and benefit to me.

In case you had illusions to the contrary, no one is sitting around hoping and praying that he will receive your sales letter. When it arrives, it is most likely an unwelcome pest. How do you earn your welcome as a guest? By immediately saying something that is recognized by the recipient as important and valuable and beneficial.

I received a letter with this warning across the top:

Warning: This letter is impregnated with a hazardous chemical activated if discarded unread. Minutes after being discarded, the letter's chemical will interact with other components in your wastebasket and explode into a giant grizzly bear that may eat you alive. For your own safety and the safety of those around you, do not discard this letter unread.

I clipped off this top panel, then threw the letter out unread. It's cute and funny, but there are better, more tried-and-true, honest ways of earning welcome guest status for your sales letter. Gimmicks too often fail. Saying something of genuine importance and interest to the recipient usually succeeds.

You say it with a headline.

Yes, I am well aware that advertising has headlines and letters generally do not. However, successful sales letters do. It can go above the salutation or between the salutation and the body copy. It can be typeset in big, bold type while the rest of the letter has a typewritten look. Or it can be put in a "Johnson box," a device presumably named after an inventor named Johnson, that looks like the one in the letter in Exhibit #8.

What your headline says and how it says it are absolutely critical. You might compare it to the door-to-door salesperson wedging a foot in the door, buying just enough time to deliver one or two sentences that will melt resistance, create interest, and elevate his or her status from annoying pest to welcome guest; you've got just about the same length of time, the same opportunity.

Exhibit #8 Johnson Box

September 12, 2005

Mr. Horace Buyer
President
ACME Co.
123 Business Street
City, State, Zip

Dear Mr. Buyer:

* * * * * * * * * * * * * * * * * * * *

Your headline goes here.

* * * * * * * * * * * * * * * * * * * *

Body copy begins here and continues normal letter format.

This book is not all about headlines, and an entire book certainly could be written about them. Instead, I've decided to give you some fill-in-the-blank headline structures that consistently and continually prove effective and successful.

Fill-In-the-Blank Headlines with Examples

They Didn't Think I Could _____, but I Did.

This headline works well for many reasons, including our natural tendency to root for the underdog. We're fascinated with stories of people who overcome great obstacles and others' ridicule to achieve success. When this headline refers to something you have thought about doing, but talked yourself out of, you'll want to know if the successful person shared your doubt or fear or handicap.

Examples:

- They Laughed When I Sat Down at the Piano—but Not When I Started to Play!
- They Grinned When the Waiter Spoke to Me in French—but Their Laughter Changed to Amazement at My Reply!

Who Else Wants _____?

I like this type of headline because of its strong implication that a lot of other people know something the reader doesn't.

Examples:

- Who Else Wants a Hollywood Actress' Figure?
- Who Else Needs an Extra Hour Every Day?

How _____ Made Me _____

This headline introduces a first-person story. People love stories and are remarkably interested in other people. This headline structure seems to work best with dramatic differences.

Examples:

- How a "Fool Stunt" Made Me a Star Salesman.
- How a Simple Idea Made Me "Plant Manager of the Year."
- How Relocating to Tennessee Saved Our Company $1 Million a Year

Are You _____?

The question headline is used to grab attention by challenging, provoking, or arousing curiosity.

Examples:

- Are You Ashamed of the Smells in Your House?
- Are You Prepared for the Next Stock Market Crash?

How I _____

Very much like How _____ Made Me _____, this headline introduces a first-person story. The strength of the benefit at the end, obviously, controls its success.

Examples:

- How I Raised Myself from Failure to Success in Selling.
- How I Retired at Age 40—With a Guaranteed Income for Life.
- How I Turned a Troubled Company into a Personal Fortune.

How to _____

This is a simple, straightforward headline structure that works with any desirable benefit. "How to" are two of the most powerful words you can use in a headline.

Examples:

- How to Collect from Social Security at Any Age.
- How to Win Friends and Influence People.
- How to Improve Telemarketers' Productivity—for Just $19.95.

Secrets Of _____

The word *secrets* works well in headlines.

Examples:

- Secrets of a Madison Ave. Maverick—"Contrarian Advertising."

- Secrets of Four Champion Golfers.

Thousands (Hundreds, Millions) Now _____ Even Though They _____

This is a "plural" version of the very first structure demonstrated in this collection of winning headlines.

Examples:

- Thousands Now Play Even Though They Have "Clumsy Fingers."
- Two Million People Owe Their Health to This Idea Even Though They Laughed at It.
- 138,000 Members of Your Profession Receive a Check from Us Every Month Even Though They Once Threw This Letter into the Wastebasket

Warning: _____

Warning is a powerful, attention-getting word and can usually work for a headline tied to any sales letter using a problem-solution copy theme.

Examples:

- Warning: Two-Thirds of the Middle Managers in Your Industry Will Lose Their Jobs in the Next 36 Months.

- Warning: Your "Corporate Shield" May Be Made of Tissue Paper—9 Ways You Can Be Held Personally Liable for Your Business's Debts, Losses, or Lawsuits

Give Me _____ and I'll _____

This structure simplifies the gist of any sales message: a promise. It truly telegraphs your offer, and if your offer is clear and good, this may be your best strategy.

Examples:

- Give Me 5 Days and I'll Give You a Magnetic Personality.
- Give Me Just 1 Hour a Day and I'll Have You Speaking French Like "Pierre" in 1 Month.
- Give Me a Chance to Ask Seven Questions and I'll Prove You Are Wasting a Small Fortune on Your Advertising.

_____ ways to _____

This is just the "how to" headline enhanced with an intriguing specific number.

Examples:

- 101 Ways to Increase New Patient Flow.
- 17 Ways to Slash Your Equipment Maintenance Costs.

Many of these example headlines are classics from very successful books, advertisements, sales letters, and brochures, obtained from a number of research sources. Some are from my own sales letters. Some were created for this book.

Tips for Mailing to Executives and Business Owners

I believe that you have to give extra concern to your letter's image when preparing mailings to executives and business owners. These people respect and generally prefer to do business with successful merchants. Remember, too, that there are intermediaries to be dealt with: receptionists and assistants who may have the option of discarding or passing along your letter. For these reasons, I suggest that you follow these guidelines:

1. Use superior quality paper and envelopes—something with a texture or watermark.
2. Avoid stuffing too many advertising enclosures in the envelope. One good approach is to put your brochures, order forms, and other essential pieces inside a second sealed package, enclosed in the main envelope with your sales letter. This presents a neat, businesslike appearance and draws attention to your sales letter.
3. Incorporate prestige appeals in your sales letter with words like:

alternative	exclusive
association	individual membership
attractive	ownership preferred
charter member	prominent
exceptional	select

superior	worthwhile
uncompromising	yield

You can also incorporate prestige in your enclosures; plastic membership cards work well.

Speaking of "Grabbing" Attention

There is a direct-mail term, *grabber*, that refers to some object attached to the sales letter, usually its first page, or stuffed in with the letter, to grab the recipient's attention. This can be as simple as a penny or piece of foreign currency or tea bag stapled to the letter, or much more elaborate gimmicks and items. In many cases, a multidimensional object is used to intentionally make the envelope "lumpy," to arouse the curiosity of the recipient. I love using such grabbers and urge all of my clients to do so.

In a mailing for one of my clients, we sent his sales letter with a miniature aluminum trash can, with a little bag of peanuts inside. The letter was "from" a squirrel, accusing the nonresponsive prospect of being "nuts," sending the trash can to dramatize the fact that not responding was the same as throwing money into the trash. This was a successful campaign for many reasons. But think about it: if somebody sends you a trash can full of peanuts, aren't you going to want to know why? That means you'll read the letter!

The geniuses at sourcing and matching great grabbers, lumpy objects, freemiums, and ad specialty items to sales letters and direct-mail campaigns are Keith and Travis Lee of 3DMailResults.com.

Tips for Mailing to the Mass Market

Bear in mind the attention span of today's consumer: it is very short! Without a car chase, explosion, or gunfight every ten seconds or so, the television viewer may well click the remote control unit and move on. That conditioned impatience carries over to your sales letters as well. You've got to reach out and grab the reader where he or she lives—immediately—then do it again and again and again. One or two sentences of less-than-compelling interest, and your reader will abandon you.

Involvement devices can help you grab and hold attention. Did you ever notice how Publishers Clearing House has you tearing out little stamps and pasting them onto the order card? Rub-off cards, tokens, stickers, and similar devices get the reader involved with the mailing.

You should also remember that color is virtually essential in consumer mailings. A number of bright, differently colored pieces are beneficial—as is color photography.

Tips for Mailings to Sell Products Directly

When you want the reader to make a decision to buy this item now—not commit to some intangible service or complicated agreement—you must follow several important guidelines:

1. Use testimonials from happy users of the product; these will do more than anything else to increase sales.
2. Remember that photographs outperform drawings and illustrations.

3. Prove that the product is easy to use. This may be done with copy, photographs, or testimonials—but it must be done!

Re. #1: I'd be remiss if I didn't mention the existence of specific laws, rules, and regulations governing the use of customer, expert, and celebrity testimonials, promulgated by the Federal Trade Commission (*www.FTC.gov*).

Re. #2: You don't necessarily have to hire photographers and get photos taken for you. Stock photos can be purchased or licensed from many different sources, such as Google. There are also all sorts of public domain photos to be found online or in other media that may be used at no cost.

Re. #3: Proof by demonstration is extremely important. I refer you to my "Wealth Magnet #11" (pp. 94–107) in my book *No B.S. Wealth Attraction in the New Economy*, and a book I coauthored with Chip Kessler, *Making Them Believe*, for in-depth information.

Tips for Mailings to Sell Professional Services

Credibility is critical here. Descriptive items of fact (such as number of years in business, number of clients served, sample client lists, and so on) can all be of tremendous value.

However, "believability" is even more important than "credibility."

The facts about your business, such as years in business, clients served, proprietary methods, and so on are important, but not nearly as persuasive as what clients have to say about their real-life experiences with you, benefits realized, and skepticism erased.

Facts and credibility only support persuasion.

Consider offering a free initial consultation or a free package of informative literature; this may break down barriers of skepticism and mistrust. Answer the question: why should the reader bother? Similarly, you should work at making the intangible benefits of your product tangible. This can be accomplished with before/after photographs, slice-of-life stories, case histories, or other examples. Demonstrate the value!

Postcards Can Produce Big Profits, Too

As a general rule, I like using postcards for consumers, not business-to-business (where there are gatekeepers ruthlessly trashing "B-pile" mail); for simple offers; and when communicating with people where a relationship is already established, rather than with new prospects.

A "Tricky" Direct-Mail Piece That Often Outperforms Sales Letters

In print advertising, there is a format called an "advertorial," which refers to an ad made to look like editorial content, like an article. There's a good example of one of these in this book's companion, *The Ultimate Marketing Plan*—look for Bill Glazer's "sprinkler malfunction" ad. These advertorials often outperform ads that look like ads, for the same proposition. One of the big reasons is simply readership. People buy newspapers and magazines for articles more than ads and are much more likely to read the articles than the ads. So the ad that masquerades as an article has a better opportunity to get a greater number of readers involved.

In direct mail, the advertorial is replicated as a tear-sheet mailing. Many of these are so successful, they're mailed in the millions, so you've probably received at least a few every year. The mailing piece may mimic a newspaper or magazine. Let's use the newspaper as an example. What actually arrives in the envelope is a newspaper-page-size piece printed on newsprint-type paper, formatted like a news article or advertorial. Sometimes innocuous stock quotes or other, unrelated articles are printed on the back, and sometimes one side has jagged edges as if torn out of a newspaper, to further the illusion. Then a little sticky note is stuck on the folded newspaper page, with a handwritten message like: "Thought you'd want to see this too, J." Everybody knows somebody with J as his or her first initial: John, Jerry, Janice. They think somebody they know has torn this out and sent it to them. They read it. Now it has a chance. When an ordinary sales letter might start out with only 10 percent of recipients reading it, this may start with 30 percent or 40 percent or 50 percent reading it. If only 10 percent of those actually reading respond, and the tear sheet starts with half, that would be fifty out of every 100 recipients, 50 × 10 percent = 5. To produce five responses, the ordinary sales letter would have to get 50 percent of its readers to respond!

Probably the person who knows the most about these, because his company produces and mails them for so many different marketers, is Craig Dickhout of Think Ink Marketing. Craig says he has coordinated the production and mailing of more than 300 million of these tear-sheet mailings! His company has produced these mailings for Georgetown Publishing, MetRX, Guthy-Renker, and Health Laboratories, to name a few. A lot of the use is by companies in the seminar, home study course, and newsletter businesses, diet, nutrition, and health product direct-marketers, and they mail large quantities to national lists. However, I've had clients in many other, diverse businesses use these types of mailings, locally, as well as nationally.

Craig points out:

"All the tiny little nuances of these pieces, and the envelopes they are mailed in, are critically important. The writing on the sticky note must appear real and authentic, not mass printed. The tear sheet must be typeset, formatted, and made to appear as an article from a credible publication, without, of course, using any actual publication's name or copyright and trademark-protected items. The envelope must be anonymous but personalized in a way that looks truly personalized."

This works extremely well but there are legal considerations. Today, the big users put "Advertisement" in small print, on both the sticky note and the tear sheet. As far as anyone can tell, it's made no difference. If you are going to use this approach, you may want to work with a printer and mailing house where someone is thoroughly familiar with its use and the laws governing its use. If you want to get information from Craig, you can fax him at Think Ink Marketing, at 714-841-2012, or visit the website at *www.thinkinkmarketing.com*.

I have a final tip about this and about any type of mailing that "sneaks up" and "tricks" the recipient into reading it: you will annoy some people. Some people resent being tricked. If you are operating in a tiny or limited market where people talk to each other a lot, you may want to be especially cautious about this.

However, the effectiveness often outweighs the annoyance factor. Personally I'm of the gotta-break-a-few-eggs-to-make-an-omelet school. In general, the best way to minimize annoyance and maximize response is to make certain you are mailing your promotion to targeted prospects or customers who will have a high degree of interest in it once motivated to read it.

ADVANCED SALES COPY STRATEGY #3
How to "Flag" a Reader and Let Him Know This Is for You

One of the simplest ways to strengthen a headline is attachment of a Flag. The Flag is brief, as brief as a single word, stuck on the front of the headline, to reach out and grab the attention of certain specific prospects, by telegraphing that the message is specifically for them. This puts the "who is this for?" ahead of what is being advertised and sold.

Here are examples of successful generic headlines with different kinds of flags attached.

Headlines *Before* Attaching Flags

- Corns Gone in 5 Days or Money Back
- Guaranteed Weight Loss Up to 15 Pounds First 15 Days—With No Exercise
- How to Have Eager Prospects Calling and Begging for Next-Day Appointments
- 28 Days to Healthier Gums

Headlines *After* Adding a Who-Is-This-For? Flag

- Waiters and Waitresses on Your Feet for Hours: Corns Gone In 5 Days or Money Back
- Disappointed Dieters: Guaranteed Weight Loss Up to 15 Pounds First 15 Days—with No Exercise
- Annuity Agents: How to Have Eager Prospects Calling and Begging for Next-Day Appointments
- Seniors: 28 Days to Healthier Gums

Another form of flagging is to focus on the "ill to be cured" or "problem to be solved."

This is usually best done by posing a question, as in these examples:

Same Headlines *After* Adding a Problem Flag

- *Foot Pain?* Corns Gone in 5 Days or Money Back
- *Embarrassing Belly Bulge?* Guaranteed Weight Loss Up to 15 Pounds First 15 Days—with No Exercise
- *No One to Sell to?* How to Have Eager Prospects Calling and Begging for Next-Day Appointments
- *Blood on Your Toothbrush?* 28 Days to Healthier Gums

Chapter 4

I Want It, but Not That Much

In retail, everybody has this experience: strolling through the mall, having an item—maybe apparel—in a store's window catch your eye and draw you in. You may look at it, feel it, want it, until you check the price tag. For that very reason, there are high-end clothing stores in some major cities' ultra-upscale shopping areas with no price tags. If you have to ask, as the saying goes, you can't afford it. You take what you want because you want it, undeterred by price, and find out what you spent much later, when your monthly bill arrives. Most of us don't shop in these stores!

Price is an issue in most sales letters, and in every sales letter where an actual offer is presented with the intent of making or nearly making the sale right then and there. Sometimes price is omitted when it shouldn't be, such as in letters designed just to get a prospect to raise her hand and ask for more information, or call and make an appointment, or come in to a store or showroom. The sales letter writer omits price, thinking its discussion premature. That may or may not be correct, depending on how heavily fear of price will weigh on the reader's willingness to respond.

If price is in play, then the complete sales letter must deal with it openly.

STEP 7: Beat the Bugaboo

Although any good sales pro will admit that price is very rarely the determining factor in a buying decision, that same pro will tell you that, mishandled, price can put the brakes on a sale before it even gets going.

The sales letter writer has to decide, before actually writing the letter, how to present price and what strategies to use in minimizing the impact of price. Certainly, if price is a key issue in your business, you'll want to minimize it to whatever degree possible in the mind of your letter recipient. Here, then are the best price minimizers I know.

Strong Resource Recommendation

The newest, latest book in my No B.S. series, *No B.S. Price Strategy*, is, obviously, all about price strategies and the effective presentation of price. My coauthor, Jason Marrs, even has a business that must compete with government-subsidized free services available to everybody! This book is, if I say so myself, the definitive guide to selling successfully at prices higher than competitors do or you can imagine, applicable to any and every product and service. Please do yourself a favor and get this book. Info about all my books is available at *www.NoBSBooks.com*.

Sell Bulk

People do equate value with bulk. One of the very first sales letters for an offer of books was for the Harvard Classics, and it proudly proclaimed its bulk: "Dr. Elliott's Five-Foot Shelf of Books." I shamelessly copied this idea for a client, with this line: "These three information-packed books weigh over thirteen pounds and cost nearly $20.00 just to ship to your door!"

One of my clients emphasized this idea in one of his sales letters, saying: ". . . and you'd better go down to Wal-Mart and buy the biggest bookshelf you can buy, for the huge truckload of moneymaking information in books, manuals, and courses that I'm going to give you, free, when . . ."

If you are selling an information product like books, courses, or subscriptions, remember that one way to convey bulk is with a list of the 1,001 (or some other huge, specific number) pieces of information contained in your product. You'll see the leaders in this field, like Boardroom Reports and Rodale, Inc. do this repeatedly.

If you are selling some other type of product, the same principle applies. Just for example, if we were writing a sales letter for an ordinary apple, instead of just saying that "an apple a day keeps the doctor away," we might list every vitamin and mineral provided by the apple, then list every health benefit delivered by each of those vitamins and minerals. We might then show the huge bulk of other foods you'd have to consume to get those same nutrients and benefits—all to turn that little apple into a huge "bulk" of benefits and value.

Discuss the Price Paid to Develop the Offer

Is this relevant to the consumer? Maybe not, but that doesn't prevent you from making it relevant.

Consider the difference between these two ways of telling you about a piece of automated industrial equipment:

Version #1

It automatically selects the right amount of material, fills the bag, seals it, and stacks it in the carton. It gets it right every time. And it is an extraordinarily durable system, good for tens of thousands of repetitions without needing maintenance.

Version #2

Our company recruited a brain trust of eight of the very best, most knowledgeable robotics engineers in the industry today to design this system. No expense was spared in obtaining the services of these experts. The prototype system was run over six months of laboratory tests at a cost of over $1 million before ever being placed in an actual working environment. In the ultimate test, we put it through 15,000 repetitions, and it performed perfectly and never needed even a minute of downtime for maintenance. You can count on this system to select the right amount of material every time, fill the bag, seal it, and stack it in the carton without error. With over $3 million worth of research and quality control backing you up, you'll finally have at least one piece of equipment working for you that is as reliable as God's sunrise.

Both copy versions describe the same machine and the exact same benefits. But the second version builds value.

Make the Parts Worth More Than the Whole

Have you ever seen the "pitchmen" at the state or county fair, with crowds gathered around them, selling things like slicer-dicers, sets of kitchen knives, or similar gadgets? These people are artistic masters at building high perceived value for each little doo-dad, each attachment, each part, so that when it's all added up it is much, much more than the price of the whole unit. The "value overage" in such presentations is overwhelming. This same strategy works in more sophisticated settings, too.

Consider the example shown in Exhibit #9. This example is fairly typical of the way value versus price is presented when selling coaching programs to professionals such as chiropractors and dentists. Its core concept is the building of very high value, then offering a substantial discount. The same concept could be applied to just about any bundle of goods or services—from carpet cleaning to wedding planning.

Conceal the Price

This is a strategy being used in print ads, sales letters, even television commercials, for a variety of consumer-product, book, and subscription offers. These marketers present prices like this: "Just three small monthly installments of $11.95 charged to your credit card."

Exhibit #9

The typical doctor saves thousands of dollars with our Full-Service System Concept for practice promotion and management. Consider the value of everything you get as a System Client:

6 Seminars During the 24-Month Contract

Each two-day Seminar focuses on a different aspect of practice success: Advertising, Referrals, Money Management, and much more. Each seminar features appropriate, expert guest lecturers as well as our Team Trainers. If you sought out individually offered seminars covering these same topic areas, you would pay at least $995.00 to as much as $1,995.00 for each one. So this is at least a $4975.00 value.

The 24-Month Marketing Kit

24 newspaper ads, 24 different patient newsletters, 24 different seasonal referral stimulation letter campaigns, 24 different in-office hand-outs ... all designed by our own advertising experts, an advisory group of 12 successful doctors, and Dr. Bill Whosis himself. We've priced this—the typical ad agency would charge more than $25,000.00 to create all of this for you from scratch!

CD-of-the-Month Club

Each month you'll receive a new audio CD for your own use and a new DVD with four Staff Meeting Starter Sessions on it. Just at prevailing prices for general-interest audio and video materials, this is nearly a $2,500.00 value. Of course, this specialized practice-building information is worth much more!

If you add up all of this, you've got at least $32,475.00 in "hard value"—in reality, a lot more—but your entire 24-month fee is only $9,895.00! And that's not all! When you join us within the next 60 days . . . before the end of this calendar year . . . you receive three very special, valuable bonus gifts and services *Absolutely free!*

First, a monthly review of your statistics and finances by our team of accountants, financial planners, and doctors, followed by a one-page report of Findings and Recommendations. Second, our famous "How to Build Community Prominence" Self-Study Course with 6 CDs, 1 DVD, and a 200-page manual . . . including interviews with seven very successful doctors from different parts of the country about their public relations successes. And, third, an opportunity to compete in our "Most Improved Doctor of the Year" competition, for an expense-paid Hawaiian vacation and exciting runner-up prizes.

While this has taken hold as a "norm" for the entire direct-response industry, the approach is not really much of an innovation; the automobile industry has been using it for some time.

I've had a lot of success with both consumer and business-to-business marketing clients, where we are able to get higher prices by disguising them in payments. For example, in one direct test, there was absolutely no difference in the number of sales generated with "$39.95" versus "2 payments of $19.95" versus "3 payments of $19.95." The third option is a higher price, but no difference! In a business-to-business situation, one piece of equipment, a $5,000.00 item, was sold in four payments of $1,250.00. I helped the client develop an upgraded, premium version of the same product that sold for $7,000.00 but was presented as "8 payments of $875.00."

The higher-priced item has a lower monthly payment than the lower-priced item—and 72 percent of his buyers opted for this lower monthly payment choice!

Three Letter Formulas That Let You Transcend Price Questions

Now let's look at three of the most effective copywriting formulas you can use to overcome a reader's hesitation on the issue of price (and on many other issues as well). These formulas relate to the price question because they get the reader to focus on something other than how much money he is going to spend—and isn't that your objective?

The formulas are easy to understand, adaptable to many business situations, and—most important—they work.

Formula #1: Problem-Agitation-Solution

When you understand that people are more likely to act to avoid pain than to get gain, you'll understand how incredibly powerful this first formula is. I have used this basic formula to structure super-effective sales presentations for live salespeople in every imaginable business, from security systems to skin-care products. I've used it for over 136 different industries, and not only for sales letters, but also for salespeople. It may be *the* most reliable sales formula ever invented.

The first step is to define the customer's problem. You may be writing about a problem they know they have or about a problem they don't know they have—it matters very little, because a good sales letter avoids assuming knowledge on the part of the recipient. So the letter sets forth the problem in clear, straightforward terms. You need to say here only enough to elicit agreement. For a letter promoting a tax strategies course for small business owners, this part of the letter can be very brief:

> You, the small business owner, are already the government's #1 tax target. Every time you look at your mail, there's another tax form demanding your attention and your money. Now you will also pay the highest price for the new tax reform—unless you discover a few secrets normally used only by "the big guys" to fight back!

If you're presenting a more complex problem, you may need to say a great deal more and add proof to your premise. I had a client I wrote a number of sales letters for some years ago who was a consultant on employee and deliveryman theft in retail businesses. Because most retailers (incorrectly and stubbornly) believe that their theft problems are with shoplifters rather than their own employees, I had to take as much as half the letter to demonstrate with facts, statistics, case examples, and other credible information that their real problem was internal.

Once the problem is established, clearly and factually, it's time to inject emotion. This second step is agitation. That means we stir up the letter recipients' emotional responses to the problem. We tap their anger, resentment, guilt, embarrassment, fear—any and every applicable negative emotion. We want to whip them into a fervor! We want to make the problem larger than life, worse than death.

My sales trainer friend, the famous (late) Cavett Robert, said to sell life insurance or cemetery plots, you have to make your customer see the hearse backed up to the door. That may sound a little grisly, but it's true.

> Here's agitation copy from a sales letter for a very ordinary product, shoes: ". . . but if you insist on just wearing any old pair of ordinary shoes, here's what you have to look forward to in your so-called golden years: fallen arches . . . intense lower back pain . . . extraordinary discomfort in golf or tennis shoes . . . even pain from just walking around a shopping mall! You'll be asking your friends to slow down so you can keep up. You'll be futilely soaking your feet at night like some old fuddy-duddy. You may even need pain pills just to get to sleep.

And here's agitation copy from one of the sales letters sent to CEOs of grocery store chains by my theft-control expert:

> The next time you look out the big picture window of your home at your beautiful, manicured lawn, think about this: a client of mine, the owner of sixteen supermarkets, told me he was doing just that—looking happily out his window across his lawn at the half-million-dollar home diagonally across the street where his new neighbors were moving in. Imagine his shock when he realized his new neighbor was the driver of the soft-drink delivery truck that serviced his supermarkets! Yes, that deliveryman was paying for his half-million-dollar home with money from the goods he had stolen from my client's supermarkets!
>
> You worked hard to build up your business. The employees and vendors stealing from you have no capital investment in stores, no bank loans to worry about, no tax forms to fill out. You've earned your success and they're stealing it from you, right under your nose! And if you refuse to see it, you are "the emperor with no clothes."

In fact, they're laughing at you, right now, behind your back. I know. I was one of them. Long before I became a security consultant, I was a deliveryman-thief! I conspired with other deliverymen just like the ones who service your stores. I conspired with employees just like the ones working in your stores. And together we stole and stole and stole some more.

If you were the owner of a chain of stores, would that rattle your cage a little? (By the way, please note that everything I wrote about the expert—whose signature appeared on the above letter—was true.)

After you've clearly stated the problem and after you've created tremendous agitation about the problem, you should have readers mentally wringing their hands, pacing the room, saying: "This has got to stop! I've got to do something about this! What can I do about this? If only there were an answer!" And that's right where you want them!

It's at that point, that crucial moment, that you whip out the solution. The third step is to unveil the solution, the answer—your product or services and the accompanying benefits.

An example of a complete sales letter using this formula is shown as Exhibit #10.

Formula #2: Fortune-telling

Our fascination with those who predict the future never ends. One very savvy public relations agent told me: "The two keys to unlimited media attention and publicity are being predictive and being provocative." Who's going to win the Super Bowl this year? What will the stock market do next? When will the earthquake occur? What will happen in the next millennium? And on and on and on.

John Naisbitt rose from obscurity to celebrity as a bestselling author, business guru, highly paid lecturer, consultant, and social commentator, all thanks to his predictive book *Megatrends*. More recently, economist Harry S. Dent traveled exactly the same path, achieving fame by predicting evolving trends. In corporate America, yet another example is Faith Popcorn, a strategic trend-based marketing consultancy.

Exhibit #10

Dear Computer Hater,

DO YOU HATE YOUR COMPUTER?

DO YOU OWN A COMPUTER THAT
WON'T DO WHAT YOU TELL IT TO DO?

ARE YOU AFRAID TO BUY A COMPUTER—
EVEN THOUGH YOU KNOW YOU NEED ONE?

ARE YOU CONFUSED BY COMPUTER-BABBLE?

In a recent survey taken by the Small Business Research Institute, over 74% of the small business owners who had purchased computers in the past 12 months felt they had been "ripped off" . . . lied to about what the computers would do for them; how easy they were to use; or the help and support available. Over 30% said their costly computers were now being used as typewriters or, worse, sitting in a corner gathering dust.

If you're in this group of frustrated, disappointed computer owners, you've literally flushed thousands, maybe tens of thousands of dollars right down the toilet!!! Is that how a savvy businessperson behaves? Of course not!

If you're afraid to "computerize" because of these problems — well, do successful businesspeople live in fear? Of course not.

We have the solution you need.

We're "PC SOLUTIONS," and here's what we'll do for you:

1. We will always talk with you in plain English. No computer-babble.

2. We will objectively analyze your needs "from scratch." We'll tell you what a computer system will and will not do for you.

3. If you already have computer equipment and software, we will:

   A. Evaluate it and help you understand it — quickly

   B. Make it work for you, if possible

   C. Teach your people how to use it

   D. If it's "wrong" for you, we'll do battle with whoever sold it to you to get it traded in, replaced or repaired

   E. If necessary, we'll modify it or add to it at the lowest cost possible

4. If you haven't purchased computers yet, we'll guide you in doing so . . . picking the right equipment and software for your needs. We do NOT sell computers or software. We're on your side!

Why suffer with unproductive computers, unhappy staff, anger, frustration? Call PC-SOLUTIONS today for a FREE, NO-OBLIGATION 30-MINUTE CONSULTATION.

1-800-DISKJOY

To prove how evergreen this approach is, I've left in the next Exhibit, #11, promoting a "crisis investing" publication. I used this as an example in the first edition of this book in 1991. If you subscribe to investment newsletters, watch your mailbox for new sales letters for investment newsletters. You'll see sales letters today using exactly the same themes as this one did more than a decade ago.

This is as good a time as any to call your attention to that recurring theme: good, solid, time-tested sales/sales letter strategies do not wear out or become obsolete. What worked in a sales letter in 1950 will still work in 2050, with only slight language modification. This is, in fact, one of the advantages of sales letters—as assets, they can have much more sustainable value than other kinds of media assets like websites, TV commercials, or even print ads.

Formula #3: Winners and Losers

Very early in my selling career, I was taught a "pitch" that reads/sounds something like this:

> Take any hundred people at the start of their working careers and follow them for forty years until they reach retirement age, and here's what you'll find, according to the Social Security Administration: only 1 will be wealthy; 4 will be financially secure; 5 will continue working, not because they want to but because they have to; 36 will be dead; and 54 will be dead broke—dependent on their meager Social Security checks, relatives, friends, even charity for a minimum standard of living. That's 5 percent successful, 95 percent unsuccessful.

Exhibit #11 Crisis Investing Ad

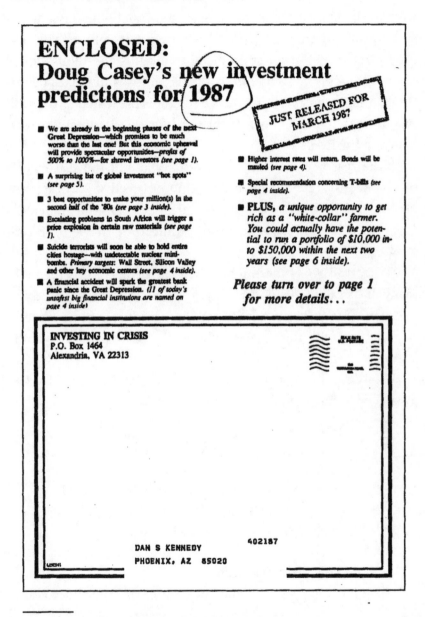

ENCLOSED:
Doug Casey's new investment
predictions for 1987

JUST RELEASED FOR MARCH 1987

■ We are already in the beginning phases of the next Great Depression—which promises to be much worse than the last one! But this economic upheaval will provide spectacular opportunities—*profits of 500% to 1000%*—for shrewd investors *(see page 1)*.

■ A surprising list of global investment "hot spots" *(see page 5)*.

■ 3 best opportunities to make your million(s) in the second half of the '80s *(see page 3 inside)*.

■ Escalating problems in South Africa will trigger a price explosion in certain raw materials *(see page 1)*.

■ Suicide terrorists will soon be able to hold entire cities hostage—with undetectable nuclear mini-bombs. *Primary targets: Wall Street, Silicon Valley and other key economic centers (see page 4 inside)*.

■ A financial accident will spark the greatest bank panic since the Great Depression. *(11 of today's unsafest big financial institutions are named on page 4 inside)*

■ Higher interest rates will return. Bonds will be mauled *(see page 4)*.

■ Special recommendation concerning T-bills *(see page 4 inside)*.

■ PLUS, *a unique opportunity to get rich as a "white-collar" farmer. You could actually have the potential to run a portfolio of $10,000 into $150,000 within the next two years (see page 6 inside).*

Please turn over to page 1 for more details...

INVESTING IN CRISIS
P.O. Box 1464
Alexandria, VA 22313

402187

DAN S KENNEDY
PHOENIX, AZ 85020

Reprinted courtesy of Agora Publishing Co., Baltimore, Maryland.

That same basic comparison has been used to sell everything from life insurance and investments to real-estate-buying schemes and Amway distributorships. I have used it face-to-face, speaking from the platform and in print, thousands and thousands of times. It quickly gains attention, opens minds, and makes people think. Then, whatever it is you are selling is presented as the path to joining the 5 percent group, the big difference between the winners and the losers.

The reason I was taught this material and the reason it is used so widely, repetitively, and continuously is that it works. People understand it. It creates fear—fear of being in the 95 percent group. It creates motivation—motivation to be in the 5 percent group.

The *Wall Street Journal* has used variations of this theme in many of its sales letters over the years. One of its most successful sales letters tells the story of two college graduates—one successful, one not, with the difference being that one subscribes to the *Journal.*

Here's an example of the formula from a sales letter I wrote for a lawn and garden store back in the early 1970s:

> Last spring, two neighbors reseeded their lawns. Now it's June. One has a beautiful, lush, thick green lawn. As perfect as the best golf course in the country. A lawn to be proud of. His neighbor, though, has a different lawn. With little brown patches. Uneven texture. Crabgrass and weeds fighting for territory.

What made the difference?

The letter goes on to tout the virtues of "lawn care counseling" from the store's owners and a particular line of lawn care products and fertilizers. It will work just as well today (in the right geographic areas—the burbs) as it did almost twenty years ago. In fact, in 1998, I recycled it for a landscaping company's franchisees, and several have reported phenomenal results.

These three formulas can be used separately or combined in a single sales letter. At least one of them and probably all of them can work for your business.

ADVANCE SALES COPY STRATEGY #4
Problem-Agitate-Solve (P-A-S) in Action

Matt Zagula, a client of mine, works in the ultra-competitive world of financial and investment advisory services, with his practice and most of the other advisors he coaches focused on seniors, retirees, and the soon-to-retire. These clients are often marketed to with offers of free dinner seminars and other free gifts to secure appointments. As I was writing this edition of this book, Matt was filling up seminars without such lures, with better quality client candidates, attracted by a strong P-A-S message.

His large-size newspaper insert, printed on goldenrod-colored paper, presents an "open letter to seniors" headlined "How Will Obama's Health Care Plan Affect You?"—and sounding this alarm: New Law Imposes $500 Billion in Medicare Cuts.

After clearly stating the Problem in his headline, he follows with Agitation copy like this:

"Programs that *you* paid for, that were promised to *you* are being snatched away from you . . . while government spending continues out of control."

With this, Matt shrewdly triggers anger and resentment on the affected reader's part at being stolen from. At this time, out-of-control government spending was a strong emotional issue, affecting the outcomes of primary elections, and polling consistently with people from fifty to seventy years old as either the number one or number two most important issue, immediately behind concerns about the economy. With this approach, he enters a conversation already underway in the readers' minds and with peers every day (see the Collier Principle in Chapter 1), and he agitates—throws salt on an open wound—a matter that easily fires up these readers. By being the one sounding this alarm about government theft of benefits the reader has earned, Matt also creates an *us*-vs.-*them* feeling, making himself the reader's ally. As further agitation, Matt invokes not just anger, but also fear, with copy like this:

"Are you equipped—by yourself—to protect your hard-earned dollars from creditors, predators, and a government gone wild? . . . Will your home be snatched away from your family by hidden medical taxes?"

This Agitation copy makes the reader uncertain and worried about what he doesn't know (which also arouses curiosity) and about his personal ability to cope with the threats to his financial well-being. It also injects the idea that his family is at risk with him, so that there's even more at stake.

This is just a sampling of the strong Problem + Agitate copy in the lengthy "open letter" newspaper insert. As the person is reading it, how do you think he *feels*? Agitated! Angry at the injustice of being targeted, threatened, and resentful of being made vulnerable, eager to stop the assault if possible, and ready for help.

When Matt has created that state of mind, he begins revealing his Solution: attending his workshop.

Not only have these sales-letter-style newspaper inserts been extremely successful, but when compared to other, common campaigns in the industry featuring free dinners, they fill seminars at savings of about $5,000.00 a month/$60,000.00 a year.

It's very important to recognize that none of this copy has to do with either investment or insurance products or financial services. It is all about the reader and her interests and concerns. The copy is also not factual or analytical, but is very emotional. Connecting with people via ads, sales letters, or any other means is best done by triggering emotional responses.

To see some of Matt's advertising and marketing, you can visit *www.mattzagula.com.* If you are a financial advisor interested in Matt's services specifically for those in the industry, call 1-800-723-0533, or leave your contact information in the space provided on his website. Incidentally, Matt and I work together, developing marketing strategies, advertisements and sales letters, and sales training for one of the largest fast-growth annuity sales organizations in America.

Chapter 5

How to Write Sales Pressure

In sales jargon, there is high-pressure selling, and then there are many other concepts talked about, like low-pressure selling, no-pressure selling, nonmanipulative selling, even peaceful warrior selling, whatever the heck that is. I've been in selling—face to face and one to one, one to many onstage and by media, and via the printed word—for more than thirty years and stand ready to insist that **all successful selling is by nature and necessity manipulative, and must apply pressure to get decision and action.** The only things people buy entirely of their own initiative and decision are basic commodities like soup, cereal, and toilet paper at the supermarket, and goods or services that respond to emergencies, like plumbing repair. Even then, toilet paper makers use labels, size variation, and price gimmicks, and plumbers often sell good-better-best options of toilets, pipes, and water heaters. Even their selling is manipulative. Certainly all other selling is.

The sales letter is handicapped by having to apply sales pressure from a distance with no interaction with the prospect, but is assisted by having the best possible pressure crafted and delivered perfectly without human variables. The sales letter writer needs to put as much pressure as possible on the reader to buy and buy now, because it is easy for that reader to do otherwise—there's no salesman sitting across from him staring him down and blocking his escape route!

Step 8 is about applying sales pressure.

STEP 8: Motivate Action

I once flew across the country seated next to a grizzled, old-time direct-sales pro who told me about getting started during the tail-end of the Depression, selling vacuum cleaners door to door. When the sales manager hired this fellow, he gave him a giant loose-leaf notebook of 299 "sales techniques" to use in getting past the front door, demonstrating the vacuum, and closing the sale. He had to memorize and be tested on his knowledge of those techniques before going out into the field.

"How many of the 299 did you wind up using?" I asked him.

"Oh, I tried 'em all," he said, "but after thirty days in the trenches I was down to using the three or four that worked."

I've had similar experiences with copywriting. Early in my career, I assembled a reference library of literally hundreds of books about advertising, marketing, direct response, direct mail, mail order, and copywriting, each full of dozens of different techniques. I suppose I've tried hundreds of them. And, over the years, I've narrowed it down to a handful that work consistently and almost universally. So, consider this an enormously valuable shortcut. If you want to experiment I guess that's fine, but if you simply want to be effective and efficient, then you can stick with these few formulas, and you can probably take care of all your sales letter needs for years to come. Here they are.

Technique #1: Intimidation

In person-to-person, professional selling, I very quickly learned the value of intimidation, and I consider Robert Ringer's bestselling book *Winning Through Intimidation* to be one of the most useful business books I've ever read. From that book and my own experiences, I learned that the hardest deal to make is the one you desperately need or really, really want to make. Somehow, the other person always senses that, and it scares him or her away. On the other hand, the easiest deals to close occur when you feel that you don't need them and really don't much care whether they come to fruition or not. This is called "taking a position," and it applies equally well to selling in print.

Here are some interesting ways to "take a position."

1. Limited Number Available

Mints, sellers of collectibles, and rare coin dealers use this strategy with great effectiveness, but it's certainly not limited to them. Many times I've used copy like this connected to a limited-quantity offer:

> ... if your response is received after our supply is exhausted, it will not be accepted and your check will be returned uncashed.

This is intimidating!

2. Most Will Buy

This technique relies on what is sometimes called the "band-wagon effect," creating the idea that a huge trend has developed, everybody is getting involved, and anyone who passes it up is, quite simply, an idiot. Here's an example of this kind of copy:

> ... thousands have joined in the last thirty days. Only a small number of people have received this invitation, and we fully expect most of them to take immediate advantage of this amazing discount—so if our phone lines are busy when you call, please be patient and keep trying. We have added extra customer-service people to handle everybody's calls as rapidly as possible.

3. You Will Buy Only If . . .

In a way, this is the opposite of #2—a challenge to the reader's ego and pride. For example:

> ... of course, it takes a very special individual to fully appreciate the value of authentic Cromwell Crystal. Even though we've been very selective in choosing the people to receive this invitation, we also realize that only about 5 out of every 100 will respond.

4. You Can Buy Only If . . .

I've had many clients who market high-priced home study courses, seminars, and tele-coaching programs on business, marketing, investing, and self-improvement, priced from $1,000.00 to

$15,000.00 and more. Many use an "application process" to make people qualify to buy. But none of them have gone to the extremes one did. At various times, he required prospective purchasers to listen to seven hours of introductory material and sign an official-looking affidavit attesting that they had done so before they were permitted to buy. Another client, a trade school, requires prospective students to furnish letters of reference.

A letter from a franchisor used the tactic this way:

> We are very particular about the people we select as business associates, so you're welcome to write or call for the free information kit, but don't get your hopes up just yet! Read everything thoroughly. Then, if you think you can qualify, you'll have to complete a detailed questionnaire, which will be reviewed by our Advisory Committee. Only if you are approved at that stage will you be invited to come to the home office for a personal interview.

5. Only Some Can Qualify . . .

This is a variation on #4. American Express has used this tactic for years in connection with its cards, particularly its Platinum Card. It appeals to the person's desire to be part of an elite group, for approval and recognition.

These five applications of Intimidation Technique are part of a broader context I teach as Takeaway Selling. It does what its name suggests: show the prospect something interesting, appealing, or desirable, then snatch it away and have it play hard to get. To extreme, it can actually reverse roles, so the buyer winds up selling the seller on why he should be permitted to buy. My entire lesson on this can be found in my book *No B.S. Sales Success in the New Economy.*

Technique #2: Demonstrate ROI—Sell Money at a Discount

ROI is return on investment. In business-to-business sales letters, it's very important to talk about, promise, and if possible, demonstrate ROI. Even when marketing to consumers, it can be helpful to show that the proposed purchase actually costs nothing, thanks to the savings or profit it produces.

Demonstrating ROI puts you in the position of "selling money at a discount." Imagine having this job to do: stand in front of a crowd and offer as many $1,000.00 bills as anyone would like to buy—for $50.00 each. To start with, most people have never seen a $1,000.00 bill and would assume you were a counterfeiter, so you'd need experts there to attest to the authenticity of the product. Then you'd need to make it easy to buy, maybe by accepting Visa or MasterCard. And so on. But certainly if you did convince them that the bills were real and the offer was legitimate, you'd have no trouble unloading as much product as you wanted! Well, that's what you can do when you demonstrate ROI.

ROI can be presented in terms of dollars to be made. For example, see this copy:

> Over 1,000 doctors reported specific increases in their incomes last year as a result of our course. Many reported net gains of $10,000.00 to $25,000.00. Once it's been repeated 1,000 times, it's no accident—it's a proven system you can

use, too. Its cost? Just $199.00. So even a $1,000.00 income increase represents a 500 percent return on your investment!

ROI can also be presented in terms of dollars to be saved. For example, this copy:

> If you paid more than $300.00 in federal taxes last year, I guarantee this newsletter will be worth at least $150.00 to you—and it costs only $29.95! That's a 500 percent return on investment, guaranteed.

It sometimes pays to exaggerate our ROI promise, then bring the reader back down with copy like this:

> ... and even if I'm only half right, you'll still pocket over $ ...

This creates a feeling of reasonableness, conservatism, even objectivity—all reassuring to the reader.

Technique #3: Ego Appeals

If everything bought in America in order to "keep up with the Joneses" were laid end to end, we'd probably have a durable-goods bridge reaching at least from here to Mars. Yes, ego is alive and well. When a product, a service, an association with a certain company, or any offer is convincingly portrayed as a status symbol, you've got the basis of a good sales letter.

There are many practical reasons for owning a fax machine. I rank it as one of the all-time best pieces of office equipment ever developed. But in talking with a marketer of such machines, very early in the game—when fax machines were "new"—I realized that my ego, just as much as the convenience of the machine, was a motivating factor in my decision to purchase. The marketer and I discussed this, and came up with the following copy:

**What Excuse Do You Make When Asked for Your
Fax Number—and You Haven't Got One?**

Can you afford to appear "behind the times" to your clients, customers, vendors, and associates? Or is it important to you to be perceived as successful, savvy, in tune with the trends leading the American business scene?

Well, that "pitch" dates back to 1991. These days, every office and many homes have fax machines and they're en route to evolutionary extinction. But I hope you recognized the universal nature of that "pitch." It has been used to sell car phones when they were new, cell phones when they were new, websites when they were new. And whatever the next, new technology is that comes along, it too can and will be sold at some point based on Ego Appeal. Again, this is not limited to tech products. You'll see it used, for example, to sell the newest innovations in golf clubs or tennis rackets, automobiles, etc.

Technique #4: Strong Guarantee

Some direct-marketing "authorities" have recently been pontificating about guarantees being out-of-date and ineffective with today's supposedly more sophisticated consumers. However, practical experience continues to prove that, one, a guarantee boosts response, and two, the better the guarantee, the better the response.

In fact, some research I've seen does indicate a heightened, harsher skepticism on the part of today's consumers. This is not just a consumer trend, but a societal one, largely supported by the repetitive failures of people we once looked up to. There's an endless parade of prominent people teaching the public to trust no one. In politics: Nixon/Watergate, Reagan/Oliver North, Clinton/Monica, etc., Obama—long list of dishonored promises, from transparency of government to stimulus spending guaranteeing unemployment capped at 8 percent, etc., etc. In religion: Jim and Tammy Bakker, Jimmy Swaggart, and most prominently and seemingly unending, the Catholic Church's protection of pedophile priests. Prescription drugs withdrawn from the market only after enormous damage and deaths. The Toyota scandal of 2010. On and on and on. Recent polls and surveys show American's trust of political leaders and government as whole, banks and Wall Street and the financial system as a whole, schools and churches, and business is at all-time lows. Skepticism, cynicism, fear abound.

My conviction is that this calls for better, bolder, stronger guarantees—not abandonment of guarantees!

Here are the best ways to use a guarantee in your sales letters:

1. Basic Money-Back Guarantee

This is the simple, basic approach: "If, for any reason, you are not fully satisfied with your purchase, return it for a full refund." I like to see this basic guarantee creatively embellished with livelier wording. You might say "delighted" or "thrilled" or even use fancier language, rather than "satisfied." You could opt for a folks-ier approach: "return the widget for a full refund—ho hassles, no hard feelings."

If it's unusual for a guarantee to be offered in your type of business, don't be bashful about saying so. For example: "Our guarantee is doubly important when you realize that no other widget maker offers one!"

2. Refund and Keep the Premium

You can strengthen your guarantee by linking it with a pre-mium (free bonus gift). Example: "If you're not thrilled with your subscription, you may cancel, receive a full refund, and still keep the leather bound appointment diary free, with our compliments! That's how absolutely certain we are that you will find tremendous value in every issue of . . . ."

3. Redundancy

Another way to strengthen the presentation of your guaran-tee is to be deliberately redundant. Say the same thing twice or even three times! For example: "Receive a full 100 percent refund of every penny you paid."

4. Free Trial Offer

You can give your guarantee a different twist by presenting it as a free trial offer. Example: "You take no risk with our Free Trial Offer! If you're not happy with the Rocket-Z Weed Whacker, just return it anytime within 90 days for a full refund."

5. Make the Guarantee the Primary Focus of the Offer

You can sometimes increase the effectiveness of your entire sales letter by making the guarantee the featured item. The publisher of a financial newsletter achieved his greatest success when he started his sales letter this way:

> Income tax savings guaranteed—or your money back! If, in the first three issues of my newsletter, you haven't found ways to decrease your taxes . . .

By the way, the use of a guarantee need not be limited to product offers. Restaurants guarantee lunch served in fifteen minutes. With a little imagination and a genuine commitment to excellence, you can find a way to bring a guarantee into your marketing arsenal.

Now let me give you an advanced technique. This requires several things: first, brass balls; second, a real understanding of the prospects and how they'll behave; and third, a strong sales message you're certain will be of significant interest to the recipients of the sales letter. The daring strategy is to guarantee the letter. I actually use this strategy a lot, for myself and for clients. Often, we'll offer $10.00, $20.00, or $50.00 if the recipient reads the entire sales letter and feels his time has been wasted. An actual sample of this is on the next page (Exhibit #12), from a mailing I did for a seminar. In this case, I paid out less than $200.00 from mailing to nearly 4,000 prospects, but I brought in over $100,000.00 in profits. And we know from "split-testing" a number of times that the addition of the "this letter is guaranteed" does increase readership and response.

Exhibit #12 This Information Package is Guaranteed ...

This Free Information Package Is Guaranteed

How can something sent to you free be guaranteed? Here's my promise: if you read the attached, admittedly lengthy letter about your speaking business and listen to the enclosed audiocassettes and watch the enclosed video, and you honestly feel I've wasted your time, just jot me a note to that effect on the back of this certificate and I'll either pay you $25.00 or donate $50.00 to Habitat for Humanity, your choice.

Since I'm sending out about 2,000 of these packages, that puts me on the hook for $100,000.00. That's okay, I can afford it. But I'm betting on your integrity as a professional colleague, and I'm betting on the fact that, even if you decide to say "no" to the offer extended to you in this informa- tion, at the very least you'll have to admit to picking up a valuable marketing idea or two you can use in your business, so this can't be a waste of time. Anyway, it's up to you. With my Guarantee, you can't lose by paying attention to this.

Sincerely,

[INSERT SIGNATURE]

DAN S. KENNEDY

NOTE: PLEASE (1) LISTEN TO THE "SPILL THE BEANS" AUDIOTAPE FIRST, THEN (2) WATCH THE VIDEO, THEN (3) READ THE LETTER, THEN (4) LISTEN TO THE "$25,000.00 A DAY" TAPE LAST. IT IS VERY IMPORTANT TO (AT LEAST) HEAR THE "SPILL THE BEANS TAPE" BEFORE READING THE LETTER.

In a somewhat similar fashion, I have a client in the financial services and asset protection business who sends out 100 of his sales letters on the first day of each month, targeting only owners or CEOs of corporations in his city, each known to have a personal net worth exceeding $5 million. In his sales letter, he suggests that in just nineteen minutes of conversation, he can reveal a dangerous "hole" in their financial fortresses or an opportunity to save on their income taxes that their current CPA, lawyer, or other advisors have not called to their attention. If he fails, he'll pay them $250.00 or donate $500.00 to the charity of their choice. With this courageous approach, he usually secures ten to fifteen appointments per 100 letters mailed (a 10 percent to 15 percent response), converts two to three of the ten or fifteen into new clients, with an average first year value per client of $10,000.00 or more.

Technique #5: Be a Storyteller

If you want to take your sales letters to an advanced level, you'll become a great storyteller.

Storytelling is very powerful, because we all love a good story. We were conditioned as children to like them—"read me a story! Tell me a story!" Fiction books far outnumber and outsell nonfiction books, and bestselling storytellers like Stephen King, Tom Clancy, and John Grisham put one novel after another onto the bestseller lists.

I usually incorporate interesting stories in the sales letters I write and encourage others to do the same. I occasionally gather no more than ten people together for a three-day sales letter writing workshop, which costs $10,000.00 per person to attend, but I will let you in on a "secret" that I teach them, right here, free!

Study good fiction and fiction writers so you can write good stories and create good story lines for sales letters. At the workshop, I include story-writing exercises.

A good example is my client Darin Garman. Shown on the next two pages, Exhibits #13 and #14, are one of his national ads and the first page of one of his top-producing sales letters. As you'll see, they tell his personal life story, a dramatic, classic rags-to-riches story.

Exhibit #13

"Former Iowa Prison Guard Shows Frustrated Investors How To Escape From Financial Prison And Truly Profit From America's Heartland!"

Darin Garman, CCIM
Consultant/Commercial
Real Estate Broker Of
Millionaires

In this FREE Report I reveal to investors with $75,000 or more to invest the easy to implement apartment and commercial property investment system, with a 10 year track record, that millionaire real estate investors are profiting from—here in the heartland of the U.S. With No Time Consuming Management Necessary—and how I discovered it years ago while working as a prison guard.

Even with a college degree, the best job that I could find after 4 years of college was working as a Prison Guard and not earning a very good living as a result. It was depressing and frustrating, at the time I wanted more for my wife and daughter, frankly, our family deserved better. So, out of frustration I searched for something better....and found it. What I accidentally discovered was investment real estate, specifically Iowa and Midwest properties. After my accidental discovery of the almost predictable profits and returns these investment properties had, I quit my job on the spot and started in the investment real estate business. That was 10 years ago. In this report I will share—

How For The Last 10 Years Individual Investors from all over the United States **have trusted me with over $151,344,433 Of Iowa And Midwest Real Estate Investments.**

That's correct. I have gone from being a prison guard to having assisted individual investors in building their wealth, predictably, hassle free and above all—profitably—Using Quality Real Estate Located In The Heartland Of The U.S.

For the last ten years I have been sharing **THE RIGHT WAY TO INVEST IN REAL ESTATE** with people as a broker and consultant. Today, I am the most sought after apartment and commercial property broker and consultant in the U.S. I have worked with many investors from beginners to millionaires to multi-millionaires, celebrities, etc. and have helped many become rich (or safely add to their wealth) using Iowa and Midwest apartment buildings and commercial property—located here in the heartland.

Now, I know you probably don't believe what I'm saying. Frankly, why should you? I'm as skeptical as anyone too. So, all I ask is that you give me 15 minutes of your time and I'll PROVE to you that I can help you build a safe and secure million dollar plus net worth (or safely add to it), using apartment and commercial property, right here in the heartland, with little risk and No management needed. **The nice thing is I found out accidentally (as a prison guard of all things) is its not that hard to do this, anyone can... If you let me share with you how, and this is important, HOW TO DO IT THE RIGHT WAY.** In just 15 minutes I'll show you how I discovered the secrets of successful commercial and investment property investors that no one really ever talks about. In fact, you will discover:

What This FREE Report Is NOT:

- NOT another get rich quick scheme
- NOT a "pitch" for some risky investment
- NOT a franchise offer
- NOT another "No Money Down" deal
- NOT an "Offering"

- Why Iowa and Midwest Apartments Are Better Than Any Other Investments, Even Single Family Homes, Stocks, Businesses, Etc.
- How To Easily Implement A Hassle Free Management System With Iowa Apartments That Frees You From Dealing With Or Worrying About Any Kind Of Tenant Problems and Complaints.
- Why Iowa and Midwest Apartment Properties Are The Best Kept "Auto Pilot" Wealth Secret Today And Why You Never Hear Anyone Talk About It.
- How To Really Break Through The Hype And Buy Iowa and Midwest Apartments For Large Monthly Cash Flow Profits With Very Little Risk—No Matter Where You Live.
- Discover The Inside "Tweak" You Can Use, Even Before You Take Over An Iowa Apartment or Commercial Property, That Can Easily and Immediately Raise The Value Over $10,000.
- How To Use The "Triple Hoop" Strategy, Only Used By Midwest Apartment Investors, To Make Sure You Walk Away From The Negotiating Table Knowing You Got The Best Deal.
- Find Out How You Can Legally Defer Capital Gains Taxes, Indefinitely If You Like, When You Invest In An Apartment And Commercial Property In Iowa...And Its Legal!

So, if you're tired and frustrated about getting your butt kicked in the market, your current income or the time its taking to reach your financial goals OR you just want to know how to **invest in apartment/investment properties the smart way, the predictable way, with superior cash flow and superior returns while avoiding costly mistakes,** this FREE NO OBLIGATION REPORT is for you. This report exposes the real strategies of successful millionaire apartment/commercial property owners and investors. **How To Get Your FREE Report:** Just call my FREE recorded message at 1-800-471-0856 and enter ID #3333. I only have 127 reports that can go out immediately so if interested delaying is not a good idea. You can call 24 Hrs. No one will talk to you.

Darin Garman, CCIM - Investment Property Specialist (#319-378-6748 Direct)

P.S. How To Get Your FREE Report: Just call my FREE recorded message at
1-800-471-0856 and enter ID #3333

Exhibit #14

Americas Top Commercial Real Estate Insider Finally Exposes The Real Secrets of The Hidden Real Estate Market No One Talks About...

"North America's Most Respected Commercial Real Estate Broker and Consultant Reveals The Secrets of Millionaire Commercial Real Estate Investors...Secrets That You've Never Heard Before"

Whether you're tired of the risk and slow returns of the stock market and other "traditional" investments or want enough cash flow coming in to quit your job in half the time...no where else will you find these closely guarded secrets to buildings wealth - until now.

Wednesday, 9:22 p.m.

Dear Friend:

My name is Darin Garman, CCIM – For the last 10 years I have been a Commercial Investment Real Estate Specialist acting as a consultant/agent for many wealthy investors. If you'd like to learn how these real estate investment secrets have broken the code on reaching your upper financial limits of massive cash flow and wealth building in a breathtakingly short time...and with a confident level of predictability...then this will be the most important message you will read in your life.

Here's my story: Ten years ago, thanks to Napoleon Hill, I decided to quit my job as a prison guard in Iowa (sounds glamorous, doesn't it?) and work in the world of commercial real estate. Actually, investment real estate. You know, apartment buildings, office buildings, shopping centers, etc.

Why am I saying that this all occurred thanks to Napoleon Hill?

Well, one day an empty liquor bottle was found in a garbage can right outside of my office in the prison. Of course I had no idea how an empty liquor bottle got inside the prison and into the garbage can outside of my office, but the Warden wanted some answers from me.

As I am sitting outside of the Wardens office, waiting to be questioned, I spot a worn out book on a book shelf. The title of the book was **"Think And Grow Rich".** Of course this is Napoleon Hill's classic.

Anyway, I started reading this book and it had a huge impact on my outlook in life. Such an impact that I quit my job there at the prison to pursue a burning desire. The desire to work in the world of commercial-investment real estate.. Why? Why would I do this?

Because I thought it would be profitable and also a lot of fun. I mean it had to beat the prison guard scene. So, being new and of course wet behind the ears, I jumped out of my prison guard job right into the world of investment real estate here in the heartland.

The Difference Was Unbelievable

I had my suspicions of how the world of commercial-investment real estate operated but you can imagine my shock at what kind of real estate outperformed all others AND how quickly this kind of property built the wealth of the investors that decided to invest in it. In other words, I was shocked at how quickly these investors built their wealth over such a short period of time. And here's the interesting thing, you never hear people talk about this kind of real estate investment – I mean in Iowa??

Chapter 6

Finally, Pen to Paper, Fingers to Keyboard

In writing sales copy, both speed and effectiveness are products of patient preparation. Everything I've had you do to this point has been about getting ready to, finally, write without pain or difficulty at relatively high speed and turn out an effective sales letter. Most people who find writing sales letters for their businesses to be too slow and arduous, and often conclude, "I can't write," fail before they write, by skipping sensible preparation. If you've invested your time properly in Steps 1–8, the actual writing will now flow!

STEP 9: Write the First Draft

This step is short because its idea is a simple one. Put what you've learned so far to work!

Up until now, the steps of the system have put you through a great deal of preparatory work. Now you can start doing what you wanted to do in the first place—write.

You can now write a first draft. Don't edit as you go. Don't worry about length, grammar, or anything else—just write.

I usually wind up with a first draft that is two, even three times the length my letter ultimately winds up being, but I prefer to get every possible persuasive idea on the table and face the editing challenge later. I think this is, by far, the easiest of the many writing approaches I've seen copywriters use.

Drop your inhibitions, sharpen your pencil, and see what happens!

STEP 10: Rewrite for Strategy

You've written your first draft; it's probably too long. Now comes the rewrite stage.

This is a difficult process for a lot of writers, including me. We need to whittle away at the masterpiece we've created to be certain it conveys the clearest possible message as concisely as possible. No, you needn't fear length. But you don't want sloppy length either. There's more to the Rewriting Step than just cutting length. In this step, we'll look at the "strategic" rewrites you can make to increase response to your letters.

Secrets of Successful Long Copywriting

"Who's going to read all that copy?" I can't tell you how many times I've been asked that question by a shocked, incredulous client staring at a sales letter that appeared to resemble a novel more closely than a note.

The answer is: those people most likely to respond.

Most research shows that the vast majority of readers never go beyond a quick glance at an advertisement, and the same is true about most sales letters. Even with excellent list selection, you'll still be sending your sales letters to a great many people who give them only a passing glance as they toss them into their wastebaskets. These people are just not interested in your product or service; they are not interested in *anything* at the moment except clearing their desks. They can't read or won't read your letter, or for any number of reasons are 100 percent resistant to your message. Worrying about whether this majority will read one page, half a page, or any other given quantity of copy is a foolish exercise—who cares? Trying to trick or manipulate these people into reading is extraordinarily difficult and of questionable value. Shortening your copy to a length everybody will read is counterproductive. Instead, you need to focus your energies on the relative minority of the letter recipients who will be interested in the message. In other words, **write for the buyer, not the nonbuyer. *Real* prospects are hungry for information.**

I have made a very fine living, made myself and clients rich, and continue to do so this very day by relying on long copy and long sales letters—8, 12, 16, 24, 96 pages long. One of the most successful sales letters in existence in the school portrait photography industry, directed at *teenagers*, is eight pages long!

There's no reason to go longer than necessary, but there is also no good reason to imprison your selling to fewer words or pages then you need to tell your best story in the best way possible. Lots of people will try to bully you out of this premise. Associates, employees, peers, friends, family, even customers will insist your letters are too long and no one will bother to read them. Unless those gifting you so generously with their opinion can match my success in direct marketing in general and with sales letters specifically or are from-scratch rich in their own right through marketing, I suggest you nod politely but ignore them and listen to me!

Strategic Rewriting

Following are some guidelines that have proven successful for developing sales letters at this stage.

Frustrate the English Teachers

My sales letters make lots of English teachers unhappy. They cringe and moan and groan. I've even occasionally received "critiques" from these dedicated grammarians. There's good reason for this: successful sales letters read much more like we talk than the way we're supposed to write. They use conversational English and popular slang. They often employ choppy sentences frowned on by stylebooks: "It's a fact. It's guaranteed. It's proven. Under the intense heat and burning sun of the Salt Flats."

Schoolbook grammar is irrelevant in the sales letter. Instead, use every weapon in your arsenal—odd punctuation and phrasing, nonsentences, one-word exclamations, buzzwords—to push and prod and pull the reader along, and to create momentum and excitement.

Have you ever been around a young kid, maybe ten or twelve years old, very excitedly telling you about some toy he or she wants, some place the kid wants to go, or something he or she wants to do? They talk so fast they stumble and stutter, rushing on without taking a breath. They never complete a sentence. And this enthusiasm is infectious. Inject that kind of action into your sales letter and you'll have a winner. Oh, and by the way—when you go to the bank to deposit all the profits your sales letter produced, nobody will ask whether you dangled a participle or split an infinitive while you were making the money.

Increase Readership with the Double Readership Path

We can divide our recipients into two personality extremes: the impulsive and the analytical. While most sales letters appeal to one extreme at the expense of the other due to the personality of the writer, we can appeal to both extremes in the same letter. The *analytical* prospect is a logical, methodical person. If she is going to buy a new car, for example, she'll make a research project out of it. The *impulsive* prospect, on the other hand, buys a new car because it's red! It's obvious that these people should be addressed differently.

The impulsive one will rarely read long copy, and, if he does, he'll read it only after heightening his interest by first skimming the letter. For impulsive prospects, you need to "telegraph" your offer and its benefits. They want to skim and get the gist of your offer very quickly. This is an impatient person, one for whom you need to create an impulsive readership path through your letter that consists of big, bold headlines and subheads; photos with captions; and boxed, circled, or highlighted short paragraphs. While reading just those things, while running along that path, your impulsive reader needs to get enough information to respond.

Frequently, after skimming, the impulsive prospect will slow down and read and consider the entire long sales letter. This is our goal.

For the analytical prospect, we can provide a more complete readership path. The Impulsive Path becomes just the signposts along the Analytical Path. The analytical prospects will read long copy—in fact, they almost require it! They want lots of facts, figures, statistics, charts, graphs, and hard information, wanting to feel that they are making an informed, considered decision.

As an aside, the letter is an interesting historical artifact, from 1990, talking about the reasons to buy silver. You might find the prices interesting. The sale of numismatic and rare coins and precious metals is evergreen. It is with us all the time, but it tends to boom at times other investments—and the economy as whole—go bust.

Exhibit #15

THE SILVER INVESTMENT OF THE DECADE

These 100 pesos silver dollars are priced to sell at only $8.75 each in quantity . . . way below normal rates. When you compare the price, choice, brilliant condition, and profit potential to any, and we do mean any, other silver coin investments, you will find this to be the best silver deal ever.

THE ULTIMATE IN PRIVACY

100 pesos silver dollars are private . . . completely exempt from the IRS reporting required of coin dealers on form 1099-B. Many investors demand complete privacy to buy and sell without a lot of government snooping . . . these coins are 100% fully exempt.

MAKE 1000% BY 1992?

Experts in many of the financial journals, people like Bill Kennedy of Western Monetary, the Aden Sisters, Howard Ruff, and others predict silver could blow the lid off and hit $25–$50 or even $100 per ounce by 1992 . . . if the financial fiasco boiling in Washington erupts. When this comes about, the 100 pesos could melt for as much as $70 per coin.

Exhibit #16

RICH IN SILVER CONTENT

These giant coins weigh nearly one ounce and are 72% pure in silver quality. The fact is, they offer 6 times as much silver for your money as BU Morgan silver dollars. And as silver prices climb in coming years, the value of these heavy coins should skyrocket. It's like having risk insurance on your silver investment. As incredible as it may seem, you can now own 6 of these big Mexican cartwheels in brilliant uncirculated condition for the price of just one common date U.S. Morgan dollar.

TIMING IS URGENT

The AMARK secret is beginning to leak out now . . . thus eliminating your chance of big profits. Don't wait until the cat's out of the bag! Buy now!! Next week or next month could be a red letter profit day for many astute silver investors who heed our advice today.

A CLASSIC FROM SILVER-RICH OLD MEXICO

As a big fan of the entire category of Mexican silver dollar size coins, I was excited when these factors came together . . . just at the right time . . . creating an unparalleled time to buy. Due to the latest Mexican financial crisis, you can buy coins at a small fraction above their actual intrinsic value—a remarkable paradox to say the least. And because this is the last of the great big high-silver content pesos coins in Mexican history . . . it's a classic!

In public speaking, there is a time-honored axiom: tell 'em what you're going to tell 'em, tell 'em, tell 'em, then tell 'em what you've told 'em. I've expanded it to: tell 'em what you're going to tell 'em; tell 'em; tell 'em again, a little differently; tell 'em again, a little more differently; then tell 'em what you've told 'em. In fact, I try to tell 'em seven times. I do this in my speeches and seminars. I do it in my sales letters, too. I call it "Internal Repetition."

In the same sales letter, you can convey your basic sales message and promise:

1. In a straightforward statement
2. In an example
3. In a story, sometimes called a "slice of life"
4. In testimonials
5. In a quote from a customer, expert, or other spokesperson
6. In a numbered summary

A "manufactured example" that uses all these methods appears here as Exhibit #17.

Move Your Reader Along with a Yes Sequence

Recently a hypnotherapist reminded me of a basic principle of persuasion: building a "yes momentum." You develop receptivity to your offer by giving your readers a sequence of "knowns" they can easily agree with and questions they can easily say "yes" to. This gets them in the habit of agreeing with you.

Exhibit #17

4 ACES CARPET CLEANING SPECIALISTS
123 Success Street
Cleansville, USA 123456

Dear Briarwood Area Homeowner,

You've probably lived in your home for three, four, maybe even five years, and in that time a lot of "traffic" has taken its toll on your carpets.

1

We guarantee to make your carpeting look like new, or there's no charge for our services!

2

Here's how it works: We'll come to your home, by appointment. First, we'll test the "worst spot." If you judge that job successful, we'll do that whole room. You continue to be the judge, room by room. You pay only for what you approve. And, during the next 21 days, you get one room FREE for every three cleaned. For example, a typical Briarwood home with an # × # carpeted living room, a # × # carpeted family room, and two # × # carpeted bedrooms will get one bedroom's carpeting CLEANED FREE!

Like new again—no matter what!

3

We were recently called to one home where, while the parents were away, the teenagers' "little party" had gotten out of control: beer stains, soda pop stains, ground-in mud and grime, and a few things we never definitely identified! Here's what that homeowner, Mrs. Trusting Parent on Elm Street, said after our visit:

4

5

"When I saw the living room carpet after the kids' party, I just knew we'd have to buy all new carpeting. I tried some carpet cleaner liquid I bought at the store, and it just made it worse. But, in just one hour, the guys from 4 Aces had it perfectly clean! I'm still amazed every time I look at it!"

Act now—call us today at 239-ACES and . . .

6

1. Schedule a FREE Consultation and Cost Quotation
2. We'll clean your carpets room by room
3. You judge our job as we go
4. You pay only for the work you approve
5. You get one room FREE for every three charged
6. Your satisfaction is guaranteed

Hank, Bill, Tom, & Larry,
"The 4 Aces"

You might incorporate this idea in a sales letter by starting or ending each paragraph with a question, or using questions as subheads. Asking questions involves the reader.

Tease the Reader at the End of Each Page

First, a format tip: never end a page with a completed sentence. This gives your reader permission to stop reading right there. Instead, always end each page in the middle of a sentence, preferably right in the middle of an interesting or exciting phrase. This spurs the reader on to the next page where, once started, he or she is likely to finish.

In addition, you may want to add "teaser copy" at the bottom of each page. This is an opportunity to use a graphic device, by the way, such as simulated handwriting or yellow fake highlight. A blurb of teaser copy is something like this:

> The author's 7 secrets for beating the stock market, revealed on the next page!

> How we saved $38,000.00 in repairs the first year—even though we were skeptics! See the next page!

Now, from these examples, did you pick up on the secret to creating good teaser copy? A teaser blurb is essentially another headline. In fact, it is a headline for the next page! So you use the principles for creating successful headlines to create your teaser blurbs, too.

STEP 11: Rewrite for Style

Beyond the mechanics, the teaser lines, and the readership paths lies the question of your letter's general strength of delivery. In this step we'll look at some of the most effective ways to make your letter stand out as "a good read."

Increase Readership by Improving Readability

What is readability? The computer industry uses the term *user friendly*. I think they apply this rather loosely, but it is supposed to mean that the computer is easy to use, uses everyday language, and does not require you to be a rocket scientist to operate it. I think sales letters should be reader friendly. That means the letter appears easy to read, is easy on the eye, uses everyday language, and doesn't require you to be a Harvard grad or a determined masochist to get through it.

A good copywriter creates this reader friendliness with a number of devices that nurse the reader along—that push, prod, pull, entice, and motivate. These devices include short, punchy sentences and even shorter nonsentences. You should also stick mostly to short paragraphs (ideally, those only three or four sentences long).

Use the First Paragraph as an Extended Headline

Think of it this way: in the first paragraph, you sell the recipient on reading your letter; then in the letter, you sell your proposition. Here's an example of a poorly used first (and second) paragraph (in an otherwise reasonably good sales letter)—and a repaired version.

Emergency Memo for Preferred Clients

I would have taken the time to write you a personalized letter, but in this instance I believe that getting the information into your hands pronto is more important. Even our Marketing Department requested I bypass them and go directly to our most concerned silver investors.

You've probably been watching the silver market lately, and as you may have guessed, market indicators show that silver is getting ready to make a surge. But many of our silver buyers have been afraid to buy bullion due to possible IRS reporting, and have asked for our recommendation as the next best thing to buy for investors who value their privacy.

Here's my rewrite:

Emergency Memo for Preferred Clients
Direct from Brent Lee, Research Department

Market indicators show that silver is getting ready to make a surge! But many of our silver buyers have been afraid to buy bullion, due to possible IRS reporting, and have asked us for help. Now we have the answer: just what the doctor ordered for savvy silver investors who value their privacy—fully explained in this important letter!

Letter excerpt used courtesy of Chattanooga Coin Co., Box 80158, Chattanooga TN 37411

Be Entertaining

No, don't be *funny*. Outright humor rarely works in sales letters and is too difficult for anyone but an experienced pro to carry off. There are safer, surer paths to follow. On the other hand, you may not want to be funeral-serious throughout your letter, either. In fact, there's no such thing as too much *interesting* copy—the problem's not with the length. The problem is being boring.

Here's the beginning of a letter I sent to a group of people who travel incessantly (as I do). As you'll see, it is lighthearted—not comical, but not dead serious.

Last night, I left a Wake-Up-and-What-City-Am-I-in-and-What-Day-Is-This call at my hotel. Maybe I'm traveling just a little too much! How about you? Just recently, I've discovered a way to earn lots of money in our business without squeezing into the big silver tube and heading off for distant lands. If you'll give me fifteen minutes of your time to read this letter thoroughly, I'll share every profitable detail with you right now!

A dead serious version of the same copy might look like this:

Tired of traveling? There is a way to earn lots of money in your business without travel. Read this letter and learn more about it.

Which is more interesting to read?

Appeal to the Senses

Although we consciously think mostly in terms of sight, our more powerful subconscious system takes in input from all five senses all the time.

I believe that the reader's "whole mind" can best be stimulated by playing on as many of the five senses as possible.

Consider, for instance, the idea of selling new business software that makes work a breeze and cuts the time required to do it by half by describing the unpleasant experience of being the last person left working late, alone, in a big, dark, cold office. Remember, your sales letter copy needs to make the reader visualize pictures and feel experiences.

Use Big Impact Words and Phrases

Consider this incredible example of words on paper that absolutely command attention and evoke emotion:

> There was a desert wind blowing that night. It was one of those hot, dry Santa Anas that come down through the mountain passes and curl your hair and make your nerves jump and your skin itch. On nights like that every booze party ends in a fight. Meek little wives feel the edge of the carving knife and study their husbands' necks. Anything can happen.

That's from the late, great mystery novelist Raymond Chandler. As a frustrated novelist myself, I love passages like that—and I have found them useful in sales letters. And if you find writing whole blocks of copy like that too tough, at least plug in "charged" phrases here and there.

Here are a few such phrases I've found or thought up and used in various sales letters:

- Serious as cancer
- Stronger 'n onions!
- Savage wind
- So overcome with frustration, he leans against the closed door of his office and silently screams
- Crawl across broken glass on your naked knees to . . . .
- So powerful (so good; so tasty; so _____) it should be illegal

Here's an example of a subhead from a sales letter I wrote for our businesses:

Why You Should Put On a Ski Mask, Lower Yourself from the Ceiling On a Wire Like Tom Cruise in *Mission Impossible*, To Steal Bill's Blueprint

This is merely a variation on the above-listed "why you should crawl across broken glass on your naked knees to . . . ." It is the same idea, delivered in the same way, creating a vivid mental picture.

I've built up a fairly large card file of such phrases, culled from advertising, television, novels, all sorts of sources. I suggest that you do the same. These kinds of phrases add bursts of color to your copy.

Resource

Reference books that copywriters use to find and create colorful, descriptive phrases:

- *Words That Sell* by Richard Bayan (Contemporary)
- *More Words That Sell* by Richard Bayan (Contemporary)
- *Roget's Super Thesaurus* by Marc McCutcheon (Writer's Digest Books)
- *Roget's Descriptive Word Finder* by Barbara Ann Kipfer (Writer's Digest Books)

Make Your Letter Reflect Your Personal Style

Some letters have personality and others don't. Some letters give you the feeling you're hearing from a real human being, a unique individual; others don't.

The best sales letter writers I know have their own unique styles. I can usually tell their work in my own incoming mail by this style, and I'm right about 90 percent of the time.

Let your own personality come into your letters. Sell in print as you would in person.

Chapter 7

On Every Road Whether More or Less Traveled, There Are Potholes

Uh-oh, a pothole. In a sales presentation, potholes stop the forward movement, and can stop the sale altogether. A pothole can be a doubt, concern, fear, skeptical response to an assertion, reason why x is fine for others but not for me, or any number of other holes into which motivation to buy may fall. Sales professionals and trainers tend to characterize all these as *questions* and *objections*.

In writing a sales letter, it's easy to get into the flow of making the best sales case and telling the best story, zipping along as if the road were perfectly paved and smooth from beginning to end. While writing, you're in the zone and all alone. Nobody's there to challenge your premise or promises. But just because you don't experience such a challenge doesn't mean your finished sales letter won't! So, Step 12 is all about spotting and filling in the potholes. . . .

STEP 12: Answer Questions and Objections

Unanswered questions and unresolved concerns sabotage sales letters! By carefully countering every possible question and objection, you put the ultimate sales presentation on paper.

The Reasons Why Not

In person-to-person selling, the prospect will usually raise one or (more likely) several objections, and it is up to the salesperson to counter or neutralize those objections effectively. Some salespeople welcome this exercise because they believe it indicates real interest on the prospect's part. Others fear and loathe this part of selling. But whatever the individual salesperson's past experience and attitude toward customer objections, they will come up in almost every sale, and they must be dealt with.

Live salespeople have several big advantages over the sales letter writer in facing objections. First, they have the luxury of responding only to those objections raised by the individual customer. Second, they get immediate feedback to determine whether they need to tell more. Third, they can "box in" the customer to turn the objection-answering process into a sure sale. There is, for example, a selling tactic known as "draining the objections," in which salespeople list the objections on a pad before answering any. They keep asking "Anything else?" until the customer runs dry of objections. Then they ask, "If we can take care of all these concerns to your satisfaction—and I'm not sure that we can—but if we can, you will then want to go ahead with the XYZ tonight, right?" When the customer says "yes" to that, he or she is boxed in. There's no way I've found to duplicate that process in print.

Our sales letter does not have the luxury of responding to only the objections each recipient thinks of. The letter has to respond to every possible objection. Our letter does not get any feedback making it clear when "enough is enough," so it must do more than enough.

I've sat in meetings with clients and advertising pros and had them argue vehemently against raising *any* objections in a sales letter. Why put negative thoughts in a reader's mind? While I avoid overestimating a customer's intelligence, I try never to underestimate skepticism! Those marketers who think they can "hide" the objectionable issues are grossly underestimating the skepticism of customers. If they are going to think of anything, they are going to think of all the reasons not to buy.

As it happens, I've had great success with a copywriting formula that airs the likely objections for the customer, then answers them. The start of that copy block reads something like this:

As attractive as this product/service/offer is, our marketing experts tell us that only about X percent of the people receiving it will respond. Although that's okay with us from a business standpoint, it still bothers me personally. You see, I know how much the owners/users of our product/service/offer benefit from it. I read their letters; I talk to them on the phone; I see them personally when they visit us; and hundreds/thousands/millions each year tell me that "(strong, brief customer quote)." Because of this, I just hate the thought of someone not getting our product/service/offer due to some error or omission in our explanation.

That's why I held a special brainstorming session with a group of our people just to try and figure out why you might say "no" to our free trial offer. After several hours, our group could think of only three possible reasons.

Here they are:

After a setup like that, I would list each reason for not buying and then respond to it.

Another, more commonly used (and, I think, wimpier, though still effective) version of this formula is to include a page of "Frequently Asked Questions and Answers" with the sales letter. The anticipated objections are phrased as questions and answered.

In either case, the answers to most objections or questions should include most, and, in most instances, all of these items:

1. A direct answer
2. A verifying testimonial comment, case history, or story
3. A restatement of or reference to the guarantee/free trial offer

STEP 13: Spark Immediate Action

When you play the sales letter game, you go up against some pretty difficult mathematics: X percent of your letters never get delivered to the intended recipients, Y percent of the letters are discarded unopened, Z percent reach people who, for one reason or another, cannot or will not respond, no matter how good the offer is. But quite probably, the biggest group of nonrespondents are those who get the letter, look at the letter, read the letter, and intend to respond to the letter—but set it aside to do "later." All too often, "later" never happens.

The Mañana Antidote: How to Get Immediate Response

In most cases, then, most of the responses to a sales letter will come in almost immediately. Yes, there will be a "trickle effect," and you will get some response weeks or even months after mailing the letter—from people who set the letter aside, buried it under a pile of papers, waited until they could afford to respond, or had any number of other reasons to procrastinate. This trickle, though, is virtually insignificant in terms of the profitability of a letter campaign. You go to the bank with the immediate response. For this reason, you must give careful thought to every possible way you can increase the urge to respond immediately.

One of my mentors in copywriting used to tell me: "Imagine your letter being read by a guy in an apartment in Cleveland, in the midst of a ferocious winter storm, with gusting winds and snow outside at thigh height. You've got to get him so excited that he'll get out of the chair in front of the fireplace, bundle up, slog through the snow, go out to his cold car, and drive down to the post office to get a money order and a stamp to send his order in—rather than take the risk of waiting until tomorrow."

Of course, the job is rarely that tough, because customers can respond to most sales letters by phone, calling toll-free numbers and paying by credit card. Still, the idea is the same. Responding is sometimes inconvenient. Usually, your letter's recipient is busy and preoccupied with other matters. There is tremendous temptation to stop at a "conditional yes"—setting the letter aside with the intention of responding "tomorrow."

Your letter's job is to get the reader to respond right now.

Here are the six most powerful ways I know of to stimulate immediate response:

1. Limited Availability

If you are honestly making an offer in which either the primary product or the premium or a discount or rebate is limited by availability, you can try to convince the recipient that "the race is on!"

2. Premiums

It is rare for the basic offer to be strong enough in and of itself to inspire immediate response from a satisfactory number of people. Because of this, I am a strong advocate of the use of premiums, and usually prefer a premium over a discount or rebate. It has often been my experience that the right premium offer can make as much as a 50 percent positive difference in response to a sales letter.

An example of both these strategies combined in a single letter comes from Bob Stupak, the creator of the Vegas World Hotel (now the Stratosphere) in Las Vegas—in my opinion, the shrewdest marketer that entire city has ever seen.

For years, Vegas World sold a package including lodging, drinks, entertainment, and a gambling bankroll for a set price through print ads, direct mail, and television. If you bought the package and went, as soon as you returned home you received an invitation to buy that same package again and use it in the future. Many people became repeat purchasers of these packages and came to realize that they could get one just about whenever they wanted it, so the usual urgency-building techniques—like an ordering deadline—no longer worked on those people. They became immune to those offers. As a result, Bob Stupak developed the letter that is shown on the next page as Exhibit #18A. Next there is a lengthy paragraph that describes the Hawaiian package. Then, the letter continues as shown in Exhibit #18B.

The next paragraphs describe the Vegas World package, making the important point that it is the same package at the same price as always.

There are several enclosures with this letter that reinforce the core offer and the premium. Did it work? Well, it got me! The morning it arrived in my mail at the office, I was busier than the proverbial one-armed paper hanger and certainly had no intention of buying another Vegas World package that day—but I stopped what I was doing, read the letter, got on the phone, and ordered immediately. Why?

1. I knew and trusted the company (Vegas World).
2. I liked the product (the Vegas World package).
3. I believed the urgency-building story (only 1,000 Hawaiian vacations available).
4. I found the premium exciting and desirable.

Duplicate those four factors in a sales letter, and you'll have a winner, too. In fact, I urge you to write those four factors down on a card or sheet of paper and keep it visible, wherever you work and will write your sales letters. If you engineer a selling environment where these four factors exist and can be carried over to your sales letter, you are virtually guaranteed success.

Exhibit #18A

From the Desk of Bob Stupak

Dear Mr. and Mrs. Kennedy:

I am writing to just a fraction of my previous guests for this first-time offer. This is a test and may never be repeated again.

6-Day, 5-Night Hawaiian Vacation

I have entered into a contract with Holiday Travel of America, one of the nation's largest fully bonded wholesale travel agencies, and have paid in advance for over 1,000 Hawaiian vacation packages to present as gifts to my returning previous guests

When you again accept your fabulous Vegas World invitation with us, we will immediately send you your documents for a wonderful Hawaiian vacation for two.

Exhibit #18B

But please remember, this is a test and is being offered to only a fraction of our previous guests and may never be offered again. This offer is available only until Thursday, November 1, or until our allotted number of Hawaiian vacations is gone, whichever comes first, so I urge you to act quickly.

3. Deadlines

The deadline is the most basic and common urgency-builder. It can stand alone or be used in combination with any of the other strategies.

If your mailings are small, you'll give extra impact with the deadline date by having it handwritten or rubber-stamped on your letter. If quantity prohibits that, you might work with your artist and printer to simulate a handwritten or rubber-stamped appearance.

4. Multiple Premiums

I've often found that if one is good, two is better! When a premium offer proves successful, it's usually smart to then test a double-premium offer.

A company selling cleaning, deodorizing, and safety chemicals via sales letters experienced considerable success when it added the offer of a free locking storage cabinet with a certain-size order received within fifteen days. When I saw the dramatic increase in response that the addition of this premium caused, I suggested testing a double premium. The company then offered one cabinet with an $X order or two cabinets with a larger $Y order. While the overall response percentage remained virtually the same, the average order size increased by nearly 30 percent!

5. Discounts for Fast Response, Penalties *For Slow Response*

This strategy is used a lot in the seminar business. Take a look at the next few seminar brochures that cross your desk and you'll undoubtedly see pricing schedules that look like this:

Enroll by January 15: $149.00 per person
Enroll after January 15 but Before February 20: $199.00 per person
At the Door (if available): $229.00 per person

This same strategy could be applied to advance-order offers tied to new, soon-to-be-released products; any kind of event tickets or passes; subscriptions or subscription renewals; and other offers.

6. Ease of Responding

Usually, the easier it is to respond the better. That can mean offering a toll-free 1-800 number, accepting response by fax, at a website, and still, by mail via preaddressed reply card or envelope included with your mailing. You might think that last option antiquated, but the largest direct-mail marketers in 2010 have reply envelopes included with their sales letters, direct-mail packages, magalogs, and catalogs.

If you drive to a website to respond or order, give careful thought to how it is structured and what the person should and should not encounter there—you don't want him distracted, confused, or delayed in filling out the order form you sent him there to fill out.

Chapter 8

Final Brushstrokes

At this point, you have turned your first draft into a second draft, incorporating answers to questions and objections and personal style, and there is what *seems to be* a finished product on your desk. Not so. There are a number of final brushstrokes needed before your work can be classed as a masterpiece. Some are small and quick. Some involve a surprising amount of work. All are important.

STEP 14: The Creative PS

Every sales letter needs a PS—do not consider your efforts complete until you have composed one. The PS can make or break your letter!

Use the PS to Stimulate Readership

Yes, many people skip to the end of the letter first. Some want to look at the signature, to try to identify who is writing to them. Others are just perverse—they also read the end of a mystery novel before buying it, and they eat their dessert first. Their perversity is your opportunity! By properly summarizing the offer/promise in your PS, you can inspire the recipient to dig in and read the entire letter, or simply add an extra incentive to respond.

PS: Even if your reader has read the text in the "proper" sequence, the PS serves as a high-impact "second headline" you can ill afford to ignore!

STEP 15: Check the Checklists

You have now written several drafts, and you've made heaven only knows how many changes and corrections in the surviving draft. If you wind up working the way I do, your draft will look like the homework you used to claim your dog ate.

For more than twenty years, I traveled constantly, some years well over 150,000 air miles. These days, most clients come to me, but still, every time I board an airplane, I am glad that pilots operate with checklists. After all, how many times have you simply forgotten to do something you know you should do? (Yesterday, I got out of my car without putting it into "Park" or turning off the engine; the car lurched against the parking block and sat there groaning, grumbling under its breath about its idiot owner. Obviously, I'm a big believer in checklists.) This step is the way to be certain you incorporate as many successful strategies, formulas, and techniques as possible in your sales letter. It is sort of a midcourse correction. You are about halfway through the entire system, the process of writing your sales letter, and this is a good time to make a number of little adjustments.

So, go back to the beginning and revisit Step 1 and the "10 Smart Questions" in it, and Steps 2–14 to be sure you've covered all the bases. Here are questions to help.

1. Did you answer all **10 Smart Questions** about your prospect? (In Step 1)
2. How many of the ten were you able to use?
3. Which of the ten did you decide to emphasize?
4. **Are you writing to your reader about what is most important to him/her (not you)?**
5. Did you build **a list of every separate Feature** of your product/offer?
6. **Did you translate the Features to Benefits?**
7. Did you identify a **Hidden Benefit** to use?
8. Did you identify the disadvantages of your offer and flaws in your product?
9. **Did you develop "damaging admission copy" about those flaws?**
10. Did you make a **list of reasons *not* to respond?**
11. Did you raise and respond to the reasons *not* to respond?
12. Did you give careful thought to **getting your letter delivered** and/or through gatekeepers to its intended recipient?
13. Did you look at, compare, and consider different **envelope faces?**
14. Did you picture your piece in a stack of mail held by your recipient, sorting it over a wastebasket? . . . and take care to survive the sort *and* **command attention and pique interest immediately upon being opened?**
15. Did you craft the best possible headline for your letter?

16. Did you craft the best possible subheadlines to place throughout your letter?
17. Did you make careful choices about your **presentation of price?**
18. Were you able to **sell money at a discount?**
19. Were you able to incorporate **intimidation** into your call to action copy?
20. Were you able to appeal to the **ego** of your buyer?
21. Did you develop and present a strong **guarantee?**
22. Overall, did you tell an interesting **story?**
23. Did you use an interesting story about yourself?
24. Did you write to the right length? (Not longer than need be due to poor or sloppy editing, but not shorter than necessary to deliver the best presentation?)
25. **Did you use Double Readership Path?**
26. **Did you use Internal Repetition?**
27. Did you **keep the reader moving**, with yes-momentum and end-of-page carryovers?
28. Did you bust up paragraphs, keep one idea per paragraph, and make the letter easily **readable?**
29. Were you interesting and entertaining? . . . **Is the letter enjoyable to read?**
30. Did you use **five-senses word pictures?**
31. Did you choose words carefully, consider options of one word versus another, and create **high-impact phrases?**
32. Did you make your copy **personal and conversational** (not institutional)?
33. Did you go back through your copy and think of the possible questions or objections it might leave **unanswered?**

... then find ways to ask them, raise them, and answer them? (Leave no unanswered questions!)

34. Did you choose and use devices to create **urgency** and spark immediate action?

35. Did you write at least one PS at the end of the letter for a strategic purpose?

STEP 16: Use Graphic Enhancement

This is a very important step—the appearance of the letter. I came to copywriting with the advantage of a commercial art and graphics background, so I have always exercised a lot of control over what I call "Copy Cosmetics," the way the copy gets made up and costumed and presented to the reader. You should too.

In recent years, since I wrote the earlier edition of this book, a super-serious student of the specialized aspect of the whole process of sales copy and sales letters has come along and even developed an amazing software system for applying the Copy Cosmetics to the copy, called CopyDoodles®. His name is Mike Capuzzi. I invited him to contribute a mini-presentation on the graphic enhancement step; he accepted, and here it is:

> **Cosmetics Matter**
> By Mike Capuzzi

Back in April of 1998, Dan Kennedy wrote those words in his *No B.S. Marketing Letter* and for me it was one of life's "ah-ha" moments. It triggered a newfound passion for how elements of copy *look* and how that *affects* readability and response.

To date, I have shared these strategies with thousands of marketers and copywriters around the world and because of this expertise, Dan has invited me to provide this presentation on graphic enhancements to show new ways you can improve the look and response of all your sales letters.

In previous editions of this book, Dan listed his twelve best "graphic devices." As you will see shortly, I've included these essential, original twelve, and added fifteen more simple-to-use— and proven—cosmetic techniques to "polish" the appearance and effect of your copy.

Copy Cosmetics guide your reader along through extended copy and provide an easy read. If your copy is easy to read, it's more likely to be read. And if it's read, the greater your chances for getting the response you want.

Copy Cosmetics will elevate your marketing above your competitors' by visually grabbing and holding the recipients' attention, which will effect a greater response, **all without having to change a single word of your copy!**

Make Your Sales Letters Come Alive

If you think about sales letters as face-to-face salesmanship in print form, you quickly understand the importance of the physical element that exists in the face-to-face scenario, which you don't have when writing copy.

If you and I were sitting across from one another, my clothes, body language, facial expressions, vocal inflections, and visual props would complement the words coming out of my mouth, with the intent of achieving the greatest possible outcome. In other words, when I have the opportunity to be in front of you, I can control *how* you hear me.

With a written sales letter (or advertisement, web page, or e-mail), I don't have this control or the ability to guide my reader along with physical gestures and visuals.

However, I can make good use of Copy Cosmetics, which transfer the physical part of salesmanship and communication (body language, facial expressions, vocal inflections, and props) to written media, through enhancements like typefaces (fonts), underscoring, boldfacing, italicizing, highlighting, margin notes, and other visual aids.

Just like you wouldn't attend an important business meeting in drab clothes and stand still with your hands at your sides, your copywriting must never do the same. Use Copy Cosmetics to make your sales letters come to life.

Earn Readership

Readership is never guaranteed. You need to use every strategy available to ensure all kinds of readers will delve into your copy.

In terms of extremes, you have the analytical reader who will read every word of your copy, no matter its length. Opposite of him, you have the impulsive reader who wants the quickest shortcut to your message.

The design of your copy needs to accommodate both types of readers, and everyone in between. However, in today's *gotta-have-it-now* mentality, most people skim long copy and rapidly decide whether or not to read it in detail.

To compensate for this, you have three options:

1. Shorten the copy, which is the path of least resistance but not the path of best effectiveness. No salesman in his right mind would do this.

2. Or, grab your reader's attention by making the copy more attractive, so that you can deliver the best possible sales presentation to every type of reader. This is clearly the better option.

MAKE IMPORTANT PARTS OF
YOUR COPY STAND OUT!

3. Use selective emphasis. Not every word of your copy has the same level of importance, so you must draw the reader's eye to critical areas, such as a benefits list, call-to-action, phone number, or website address.

Copy Cosmetics are extremely helpful for grabbing attention and guiding your reader's eyes to important areas in your copy. I call this **selective emphasis**. A proven and easy way to do this is with handwritten marginal notes and hand-drawn doodles. These are great eye-magnets and should be used around important areas of your copy.

How Much Is Too Much?

Now that you are starting to understand the importance of Copy Cosmetics, you may be wondering if it's possible to overuse these powerful enhancements. The answer: *Yes.*

Before I share my list of the twenty-seven essential Copy Cosmetic techniques, I must provide this warning: Like anything done in excess, Copy Cosmetics are no different. If you use too many within a single sales letter, you will only distract the reader. Remember, when *everything* is emphasized, *nothing* stands out.

At the end of this chapter, I will show you eight real-world examples of effective use of Copy Cosmetics (and give you the opportunity to download them for free, along with my detailed commentary on each). So, with all that in mind, here—in alphabetical order—are my . . .

27 Essential Copy Cosmetic Enhancements

1. **Boldfacing**—Use **bold** type to emphasize subheadings, important words, phrases, dates, and other segments of important copy. Bold type instantly draws attention to

these important points and allows your reader to skim the critical content.

> 2. Borders—Borders draw attention to important items such as headlines, testimonials, and coupons. A red border around a coupon grabs attention. Consider adding borders to your guarantees to make them look even more valuable. Use borders around light-colored illustrations, graphics, charts, and photos to help set them apart.

3. CAPITALIZATION—Use capitalization to set off a single (or two or three) word(s) which need extra emphasis. Use *sparingly*, since oftentimes it's perceived as "shouting."

4. Captions—These should always be used under illustrations, graphics, charts, and photos, because captions are one of the most often read Copy Cosmetic enhancements when placed next to an attention-grabbing image.

5. Cartoons, Comics, and Caricatures—These little beauties are among the least used, but most effective, ways to grab attention and lighten up your copy. To get an additional boost in response, personalize the caption with the recipient's name (more on "Personalization," below).

6. Color—Blues and softer colors relax us; reds and hotter colors energize us. Use strong colors to grab attention and create urgency (I prefer red). Be careful you don't use too many colors, which will distract your reader.

Also, understand the concept of "reverse print" (light copy on a dark background) and be very careful to not overuse it.

7. Columns—50- to 70-character-wide columns are easier to read than single, wide columns. Look at your newspaper and classic direct-response advertisements to see how they use columns to "air out" the copy.

8. Drop Caps—An enlarged, initial capital draws the reader's eye to the beginning of your letter. Studies show this simple technique increases readership.

9. Fonts and Typefaces—Whole books have been written about this enhancement alone. Here's the simple rule for maximum readability: Use **serif fonts** (serifs are the short curls at the tops and bottoms of letters)—for example, Times Roman, Courier—for print marketing, and use **sans-serif fonts**—for example, Arial, Verdana—for online marketing. *Consider using handwriting fonts for added personality.*

10. Highlighting—This adds a touch of realism and color. Use highlights to emphasize key copy. Be careful not to overuse. (When *everything* is emphasized, *nothing* stands out.) Yellow highlighting mimics what you would do by hand with a yellow highlighter pen.

11. Indenting—Indentation of paragraphs makes for easier reading and helps break up long copy.

12. *Italics*—Use italics to create emphasis on a word or short phrases. Italicizing creates urgency and intensity. Always use italics for book titles.

13. Line Justification—Justified text is typically harder to read (where both the left and right margins line up, like this book) and should not be used in your sales letters. Instead, use flush left and ragged right. An exception to this rule is multicolumn advertisements and newsletters.

14. Line Spacing—This is critical for maximum readability. Proper line spacing is based on typeface, font size, and line length. Wider sections of copy should have more spacing to enhance readability.

15. Lists—Include bullet, number, and checklists among your copy. This is an important technique because it communicates priority and "airs out" your copy.

16. Personalization—Personalization is a critical Copy Cosmetic strategy, because it can yield significant bumps in customer response, much more than simply inserting the reader's name in the salutation. Consider personalizing your headline and response device (e.g., certificate or fax-back form). Always sign your letters by hand—or add a graphic signature in blue—for an added personal touch.

17. Photographs and Illustrations—Studies have shown that photos and illustrations are two of the most-often looked-at parts of a letter and help to increase interest, because people love looking at compelling photos. Con-

sider photos of products in use, close-ups, before-and-after, people, and pets. Always include a caption.

18. Screen Tints—Use screen tints to draw attention to specific areas of copy. This gives the appearance of more than one color when doing one-color printing. Use light backgrounds for maximum readability.

19. Short Words, Sentences, and Paragraphs—Short. Delivers. Punch. Short grabs attention, helps keep the reader reading, and effectively breaks up long copy.

20. Sidebars—Sidebars help hold together—and differentiate—blocks of copy. They are excellent for case studies, testimonials, and product highlights.

21. Simulated Hand-Drawn Doodles—A.k.a. CopyDoodles®. Simulated hand-drawn doodles help draw the reader's eyes to important areas of your copy, add variety and interest to the eye and brain, and create a more personal reading experience.

22. Simulated Handwritten Margin Notes—These margin notes add a unique, "me to you" look. They generate interest and grab attention. All the great copywriters agree that handwritten margin notes can increase response. Use CopyDoodles® to add high-quality handwritten enhancements quickly and easily.

WOW!

23. Simulated Rubber  —A favorite technique of mine, especially on envelopes and order forms. They help create an attention-grabbing, unique, one-of-a-kind look.

24. Subheads—Subheadings break up long copy and offer eye relief. They are also critical for skimmers and make long copy less imposing. They should be written as "breadcrumbs" to draw and entice the reader to follow you along your copy. Format—font style, size, and bolding—is a critical consideration to ensure maximum readability of subheads.

25. Text Boxes—A powerful way to draw the eye to important areas of information. Consider using text boxes for testimonials, offers, and guarantees.

26. Underscoring—This Copy Cosmetic technique allows you to emphasize keywords or phrases. Always underscore with a continuous line. Use to signify e-mail and web addresses. Use sparingly, since overuse distracts and distances the reader from your content and can decrease readability.

27. White Space—This is necessary for readability; too much and you lose valuable real estate; too little and the content is difficult to read. Add white space around headlines and images for maximum impact.

> **Resource!**
>
> For a more detailed presentation of my "27 Copy Cosmetic Techniques," including the color examples found at the end of this step, and my commentary on how each uses these powerful techniques, visit *www.copycosmetics.com*.

A "Brilliant" Tool for Anybody Writing Copy

In 2007, my passion for helping others to improve the look and response of their copy and marketing resulted in the release of a copywriting tool that I created for my own business and clients. At the time, it was a small collection of a few hundred handwritten "response triggers" and doodles.

With the positive support of folks like Dan Kennedy (who called them "brilliant"), Ted Nicholas, Bill Glazer, and several other exceptional copywriters, I offered my CopyDoodles® to the world. Since then, the "art of copywriting" has never been the same.

Thousands of professional copywriters, business owners, professional practice owners, and entrepreneurs use CopyDoodles® to improve the look and response of their copywriting and marketing projects. CopyDoodles® are *super*-easy to use, and within seconds you can dramatically improve the personality and scannability of your sales letters. Plus, they make copywriting *a lot more fun!*

Today, CopyDoodles® is the world's largest collection of hand-drawn and handwritten graphics and software tools for business owners looking to improve their response, with more than 7,000 unique graphics available via instant download from our CopyDoodles® Access Club. This one-of-a-kind website is *the* go-to resource for smart copywriters.

Resource!

For a *free* CopyDoodles Starter Kit and swipe file valued at $97.00, visit *www.copycosmetics.com.*

Exhibit #19 Direct-Mail Postcard

Exhibit #20 Direct-Mail Letter

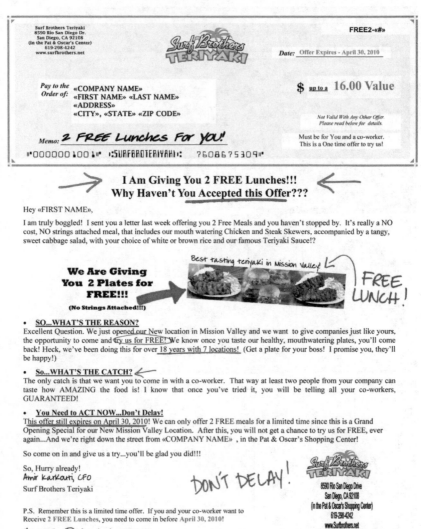

Surf Brothers Teriyaki
8590 Rio San Diego Dr.
San Diego, CA 92108
(in the Pat & Oscar's Center)
619-298-4242
www.surfbrothers.net

FREE2-«#»

Date: Offer Expires - April 30, 2010

Pay to the Order of: «COMPANY NAME»
«FIRST NAME» «LAST NAME»
«ADDRESS»
«CITY», «STATE» «ZIP CODE»

$ up to a **16.00 Value**

Not Valid With Any Other Offer.
Please read below for details.

Memo: **2 FREE Lunches For YOU!**

Must be for You and a co-worker.
This is a One time offer to try us!

⑈000000 100 1⑈ ⑆5URFBROTERIYAKI⑆ 7608675309⑈

I Am Giving You 2 FREE Lunches!!!
Why Haven't You Accepted this Offer???

Hey «FIRST NAME»,

I am truly boggled! I sent you a letter last week offering you 2 Free Meals and you haven't stopped by. It's really a NO cost, NO strings attached meal, that includes our mouth watering Chicken and Steak Skewers, accompanied by a tangy, sweet cabbage salad, with your choice of white or brown rice and our famous Teriyaki Sauce!?

We Are Giving You 2 Plates for FREE!!!

(No Strings Attached!!!)

Best tasting teriyaki in Mission Valley!

FREE LUNCH!

- **SO...WHAT'S THE REASON?**
Excellent Question. We just opened our New location in Mission Valley and we want to give companies just like yours, the opportunity to come and try us for FREE! We know once you taste our healthy, mouthwatering plates, you'll come back! Heck, we've been doing this for over 18 years with 7 locations! (Get a plate for your boss! I promise you, they'll be happy!)

- **So...WHAT'S THE CATCH?**
The only catch is that we want you to come in with a co-worker. That way at least two people from your company can taste how AMAZING the food is! I know that once you've tried it, you will be telling all your co-workers, GUARANTEED!

- **You Need to ACT NOW...Don't Delay!**
This offer still expires on April 30, 2010! We can only offer 2 FREE meals for a limited time since this is a Grand Opening Special for our New Mission Valley Location. After this, you will not get a chance to try us for FREE, ever again...And we're right down the street from «COMPANY NAME» , in the Pat & Oscar's Shopping Center!

So come on in and give us a try...you'll be glad you did!!!

So, Hurry already!
Amir Karkouti, CFO
Surf Brothers Teriyaki

DON'T DELAY!

8590 Rio San Diego Drive
San Diego, CA 92108
(in the Pat & Oscar's Shopping Center)
619-298-4242
www.Surfbrothers.net

P.S. Remember this is a limited time offer. If you and your co-worker want to Receive 2 FREE Lunches, you need to come in before April 30, 2010!

DUE BY April 30, 2010

HERE'S SOME OF OUR CUSTOMERS:

Exhibit #21 Direct-Mail Postcard

"Announcing A Brand New Social Networking Website Dedicated to Barbecue Enthusiasts Around The World!"...

"At Last, Here's A 100% Risk-FREE And Guaranteed Way To Take The "Guess Work" Out Of Making A Killing In Business With Barbecue!"...

"And...If You're Smart, You Can Find Out How YOU Can Easily Do All Of This (And More)!"

Dear Friend,

If you want to *"get in"* on this ground floor opportunity marketing to a steady stream of frenzied, highly identifiable and easily targeted customers then this will be the most exciting message you will ever read!

It's true! The popularity of southern style barbecue and online networking communities has sky-rocketed! Millions of "wanna-be" pit bosses flock to barbecue competitions, cooking schools and online forums to share ideas, debate topics and

The # 1 Virtual Gathering Place For Barbecue Enthusiasts

just to "hang out" in the place they belong.

Look, barbecue has become big business. An estimated 11.6 million grills were shipped to retailers last year. There are some 2.9 BILLYUN barbecue events held annually in the world and at least 8 out of 10 Americans own some sort of barbecue grill—in fact, *"New York Magazine"* has called Barbecue the "NEW" Deli.

BBQFreaks.com is still in it's "beta test" stage so this is a great opportunity for you to craft your message for this highly rabid market place.

" You shouldn't ignore the <u>EXPLOSIVE</u> growth in popularity and financial success of online community sites"...

" You shouldn't ignore the EXPLOSIVE growth in popularity and financial success of online community/social/ Business/ special interests networking sites. It's my belief that elements of myspace, Facebook, YouTube, etc should be incorporated into every info-marketer's online communities...for "Stickiness" and for equity"
-Dan Kennedy, March 2008, No B.S. Info-Marketing Letter

OVER. PLEASE

"How To Make A Killing Marketing to Barbecue Freaks!"...

Are You Aware Of These 7 Reasons Why You're Missing The Boat If You're <u>Not</u> Marketing To Barbecue Enthusiasts?"...

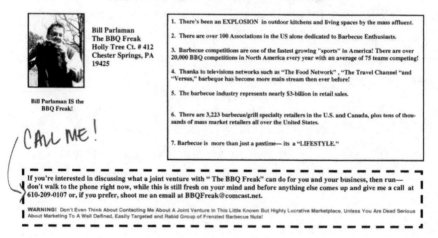

Bill Parlaman
The BBQ Freak
Holly Tree Ct. # 412
Chester Springs, PA
19425

Bill Parlaman IS the BBQ Freak!

CALL ME!

1. There's been an EXPLOSION in outdoor kitchens and living spaces by the mass affluent.

2. There are over 100 Associations in the US alone dedicated to Barbecue Enthusiasts.

3. Barbecue competitions are one of the fastest growing "sports" in America! There are over 20,000 BBQ competitions in North America every year with an average of 75 teams competing!

4. Thanks to televisions networks such as "The Food Network" , "The Travel Channel "and "Versus," barbeque has become more main stream then ever before!

5. The barbecue industry represents nearly $3-billion in retail sales.

6. There are 3,223 barbecue/grill specialty retailers in the U.S. and Canada, plus tens of thousands of mass market retailers all over the United States.

7. Barbecue is more than just a pastime— its a "LIFESTYLE."

If you're interested in discussing what a joint venture with " The BBQ Freak" can do for you and your business, then run— don't walk to the phone right now, while this is still fresh on your mind and before anything else comes up and give me a call at 610-209-0107 or, if you prefer, shoot me an email at BBQFreak@comcast.net.

WARNING! Don't Even Think About Contacting Me About A Joint Venture In This Little Known But Highly Lucrative Marketplace, Unless You Are Dead Serious About Marketing To A Well Defined, Easily Targeted and Rabid Group of Frenzied Barbecue Nuts!

Exhibit #22 Web Option

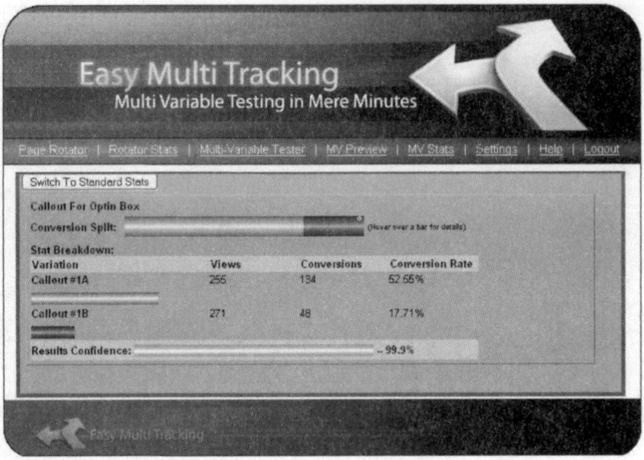

This is a screenshot of a piece of software that split-tests various components of websites. In this screen, you are seeing the results of the web option form with and without "Grab Your Copy Now" CopyDoodle.

Callout #1A—with the CopyDoodles—256 people viewed the form and 134 people opted in.

Callout #1B—without the CopyDoodle—271 people viewed the form, but only forty-eight opted in.

This is a difference of 179 percent and shows you the power of a simple cosmetic enhancement.

STEP 17: Rewrite for Passion! Edit for Clarity!

Here is yet another chance to rewrite your piece; this time the accent is on the unpredictable, passionate side of your offer.

How to Put Passion Into Your Sales Letter

Sales letter writing is no place for pure, cold, hard logic, even if you are selling a logical proposition to presumably logical people. I don't care what business you're in or who your prospects or customers are, they buy by emotion and then justify their choice with logic. My speaking colleague, the famous sales trainer and motivational speaker Zig Ziglar, calls that "emotional logic."

Even in very technical fields, you do not find too many hardcore analytical personalities in sales positions. These "cold fish" just can't make it in selling. Most successful salespeople, again—even in highly technical fields—have amiable, friendly, enthusiastic personalities. They are "people people." This gives us valuable clues about the necessary personality of a sales letter.

"Cold fish" sales letters rarely work. The purely factual approach fails almost every time it's used. A sales letter needs an enthusiastic personality—and because it is ink on paper, not warm flesh and blood, the letter has to work harder at being enthusiastic. That means that what will seem overly expressive when you write it will still wind up understated when it's read.

No matter what people may think about their own attention spans or those of their prospects, the number one sin in marketing in general (and sales letter writing in particular) is being boring. The desirable opposite, I think, is being exciting, passionate—even a little wild! Are you eager to pull the passion from within yourself—to channel it into your sales letter? Here's an exercise I suggest you try: Assume you're writing a letter to someone with whom you're having an illicit affair. In the letter, you're going to convince your lover—who is slightly more conservative than you are, but who has shown signs of having a wild side—to take an entire week off to be with you. You must convince the person to make some excuse to be away from work and responsibilities for that week, to take all the risks inherent in this action in order to sneak away to the Bahamas with you—where you will have free use of a friend's villa, right on the beach. Use as many pages as you like. (You've got a sales job and a half here!)

You can be bold, daring, even shocking. You can be poetic; you can be romantic; you can be colorful in your descriptions of the sun, the sea, the land, the stars, the breeze, the ocean smell. Where will you go? What will you do when you get there? Anticipate the objections and eliminate them as you go. Make huge promises! Create an overwhelming desire in your reader to go with you on that trip—no matter what the risk!

I conducted this exercise in a direct-marketing seminar once; everyone in the group was participating eagerly except for one man. He came up to me after the seminar and told me he'd had problems with the whole idea.

"First of all," he said, "I've been married to the same woman for thirty-eight years. In all that time, I haven't even thought about an affair. And there's certainly nothing exciting about my relationship. Second, I own a specialty electronic-parts business. We sell parts to manufacturers of electronic products. Our business is boring and so is theirs. We talk to each other in part numbers. No romance there. I don't think this is for me."

As I quizzed him about his business, I found that his was one of about a dozen similar companies in this funny little industry, all pursuing the same clientele—in, incidentally, the same dull, dreary, traditional way. The only two things his customers supposedly cared about were price and reliable, on-time delivery.

I'm a little embarrassed to admit it, but I took this fellow out after the seminar to a rather raucous bar and popped a few drinks into him. I wanted to loosen him up, try to get his motor revving. I challenged him to come up with a passionate, lively sales letter to send to companies he didn't have as customers, and to send just ten or twenty at a time.

He came back a couple of months later, the proud and happy creator of a marketing revolution in his once-dreary little industry. His sales letter was printed in red ink, on hot-pink paper, with the headline:

**69 Things You Can Do After Work
When You Are Absolutely Free of Worry
About Whether or Not Your Part
Will Arrive On Time Tomorrow.**

In the first paragraph, he quickly told the reader about his huge inventory, twenty-four-hour-a-day ordering service, air-courier shipments, and guarantee of on-time delivery. The rest of the three-page letter was, sure enough, devoted to a list of 69 things a worry-free manager might do with an evening. Some were funny; some were ordinary, but pleasant; some were outrageous; a few were a little "blue." Enclosed with the letter was a copy of his regular parts catalog with a huge hot-pink sticker affixed to the front: *"Boring but Necessary."*

"Well," he said proudly, "what do you think?"

What do you think? Frankly, I was afraid he was going to tell me a horror story about how he had mailed these things and been laughed out of town. But the truth was, he'd sent out 100 of these pink-and-red motivators, gotten twenty-two telephone calls from amused (and amazed) recipients, and received eighteen separate first-time orders, all of which converted to long-term accounts. The campaign was worth over $200,000.00 in new business to him that year.

Although his situation was unique, the episode introduces a valuable lesson about putting passion into a sales letter: no matter what your business may be, you can find something to get excited about. **If you can't romanticize your product or service or its direct benefits, you've got to be able to create excitement out of the feelings of owning it or using it, or the enjoyment of the money or time it saves. Find something for the reader to get excited about!** It doesn't matter what your topic is: there is a way to give your sales story a passion injection.

Consider Exhibit #23.

Exhibit #23

WHEN ARE YOU DOING TO GET TIRED ENOUGH OF BEING IN DEBT TO DO SOMETHING ABOUT IT?

Dear Friend,

You're getting this letter because—incredibly—it's a matter of public record that you're in financial difficulty!!! I say "dear friend," because six years ago, I was where you are now . . . embarrassed. Frustrated. Hounded by creditors. Paranoid. Defensive. Angry. Wondering whether I'd ever get ahead. Hating the ring of the phone.

That experience motivated me to become a researcher. In one year, six years ago, I spent over 300 hours at the public library, at the law library, interviewing accountants and CPAs and tax experts and attorneys. From all that, I developed a nine-point step-by-step strategy for getting out of debt once and for all. It worked for me. I can work for you. Here are some of the nine steps:

1—STOP creditors' collection actions (in 90% of the cases, without bankruptcy, without an attorney!)

3—PROTECT your personal and family property from creditors

5—"DAMAGE CONTROL" for your credit rating and credit reports, so you can rebuild fast

7—Establish a spare time, weekend, 2nd income of $300 to $500 per month, from your choice of a dozen different proven plans

All nine of my steps can save your financial life!

My information will stop the wolves from barking at your door . . . protect your possessions . . . give you time to breathe and think . . . reorganize your payments to an amount you really can handle . . . put more money in your pocket . . . give you knowledge, control, confidence and peace of mind. How about a good night's sleep—for a change? Here I am, my friend . . . at the end of the tunnel . . . shining a beacon of light back toward you, saying "C'mon, let me help you escape your Debt Trap!"

Right now, you can hear all about my nine step system just by making a simple telephone call to 1-900-000-0000. I've recorded a message especially for you! You'll hear my personal debt-to-riches story . . . how my strategy works . . . and how you can get and try it yourself on a satisfaction guaranteed basis. There is a charge for the call: $2.00 for the first minute and $1.00 for each additional minute which will appear on your phone bill—but this is a very small cost to invest in getting debt free!

Aggressive Editing

Now that we've added a splash of color and passion, it's time to get a little ruthless with your text. Aggressive editing means cutting out every word or phrase that fails to advance, strengthen, or reinforce your basic sales story. You're not editing to shorten. You are editing to clarify, and that will automatically shorten the letter.

For example, a sales letter draft had this wording:

> We have many imitators, but no one who matches the quality of our products, our eight years of leadership in this industry, or our guarantee. . . .

In the aggressive editing process, this was changed to:

> Our many imitators can't match . . .

See how much faster that gets to the point? How much clearer it makes the letter?

This process takes days. You may need to attack your text, set the draft aside, then come back to it hours later and edit some more. But do it!

Advice from the terrific novelist Elmore Leonard:
Cut out the parts the reader tends to skip

STEP 18: Compare Your Draft to Examples

I like to put my draft side by side with good examples, to compare and check for ways to improve my letter. This book is full of examples useful for this purpose.

Don't just use one letter for comparison—find several that allow you to isolate your word's strengths and weaknesses.

Does your letter's text flow as smoothly as the letters referenced? Is it as compelling? Does it speak to its target audience as well? Is it structurally as sound? Is it as easy to understand? Does it excite a potential reader to action as effectively?

When you've spent a good chunk of time reviewing how your letter stands up to the others reproduced in this book, consider incorporating changes and revisions based on your observations.

Chapter 9

The End Is Near

Are we *ever* going to get this thing in the mail? Yes. Very soon. But before we do, let's take just a few extra steps to give it the best chances of success possible. A pilot does a final walk around the plane, then a final check of all the gauges and functions before rolling down the runway to take off.

STEP 19: Pretest

No-Cost Pretesting

These days even a relatively small direct-mail test of, say, 5,000 to 10,000 units can cost a small fortune. That's why I like to pretest (at a cost of $0, of course). I find glitches that can still be repaired before mailing, and get a better feel for the probable success or failure of the letter. In a few cases, the pretest feedback has been so bad that I've trashed the entire letter and started over. In most cases, nothing that drastic happens, but a few final opportunities for improvement are detected.

The following are the best no-cost ways to pretest a sales letter.

Read the Letter Aloud

It should "flow" smoothly, conversationally, whether read silently or aloud. If you find tongue twisters or hang-ups, fix them. The sales letter must read easily.

Read the Letter to Several People Who Might Be Typical Customers for the Offer

I know one highly paid copywriter of sales letters geared to blue-collar men. He routinely takes his letters down to a neighborhood bar, buys a round of beers for everybody, and then reads them his sales letter drafts. He welcomes their comments and ideas. But he's more interested in the secret acid test they have no idea they're participating in. If some of them start asking how they can get the product or service described in the letter, he knows the basic approach is sound. If the letter is exciting enough to move people from the critic's corner to the cash-register line, he knows he's got a winner.

Sometimes this type of input can lead to dramatic results. I gave one client's direct-mail package—a short letter, a full-color catalog, and a response device—to a few typical customers; they looked through it all, but then they had a zillion questions. So the good news was: it got some motors running. The bad news was: it left lots of unanswered questions that could prevent response. As a result, I created a new eight-page sales letter that answered all of their questions. Response is up almost 15 percent since the use of the new letter began.

Have a Young Child Read the Letter Aloud to You

Any words or phrases the youngster has difficulty with should probably be changed. I've used this strategy for many years; however, it is now more important than ever.

I know that many will instantly object to this idea. Perhaps you think your customers are "smarter than the average bear." If so, consider an article from *DM News* headlined: "Look Who's Opening Your Direct Mail—and Can They Read It?" It reads, in part, as follows: "Over 27 million adults cannot read. An additional 46 million are either functionally illiterate or marginally illiterate. This means that one out of every three adult Americans lacks a skill level required to be satisfactorily literate in today's society."

Of course, the important question is: are your customers literate? The article goes on: "Many marketing professionals feel that this incidence of illiteracy does not pertain to their own potential customers, particularly when mailing business-to-business. A word of caution: Illiteracy is not restricted to those standing in the unemployment lines. . . . Sadly, perhaps, corporate America, in order to fill available job openings, has found it necessary to lower its employment requirements. Others who are illiterate have found ways to bypass the system and secure employment without detection."

It's my most current, admittedly curmudgeonly observation that the younger-than-thirty crowd is even less literate and cursed with poorer attention spans than the rest of us. If you are writing to Gen'-X'ers and younger, all too often you are writing to nonreaders.

I believe that mysterious failures of creatively and technically sound sales letters may very well be due, at least in part, to this large, growing, and somewhat hidden functional illiteracy. This is a strong mandate for lowest-common-denominator copywriting.

Beyond the straightforward illiteracy issue is what I call the Sophistication Trap: stubbornly believing that your customers are more sophisticated than they really are.

Some of the most talented, highly skilled, and best-paid copywriters on the planet create the full-page, copy-intensive direct-response ads that appear in the *National Enquirer* and similar tabloids. Some of these copywriters earn fees and royalties of $25,000.00 to $100,000.00 per ad. To command that kind of money, you just have to be good. And for an advertiser to pay that kind of money, there have to be outstanding results. So if you want to go to a school of profitable copywriting tutored by the best and the brightest, pick up a copy of the *National Enquirer*. Skip the articles about the invading Martians impregnating talk show hosts—but study the ads!

If you choose to stick with the bias that your customers are much smarter and more sophisticated than that, I believe that choice will cost you a great deal of money.

First of all, there are a lot of closet *National Enquirer* readers out there—just take a look at the circulation figures! Second, no matter who your customers are, they are part of the buying public reached and swayed by TV commercials, which are now geared to a sixth-grade reading level. Butcher, baker, candlestick maker, doctor, lawyer, CEO—they're all people who respond to the same basic motives and appeals. And the keyword there is *basic*.

Regardless of who you are addressing your copy to, it is better to err on the side of simplicity. (Bear in mind the remark attributed to P. T. Barnum about how no one ever went broke overestimating the ignorance of the American public. Lots of people have gone broke overestimating the sophistication of their customers.)

STEP 20: Bring Your Letter to Life

Finally—you're free to have your edited draft prepared exactly as you intend to send it out. In other words, you can now pretend you are getting it ready for the printer. Think of this is your "dry run" or "dress rehearsal."

This is an exciting step because your letter comes to life before your eyes! What do you think of the current state of your project?

STEP 21: Change Graphic Enhancements

Meet with your typesetter, layout artist, and printer to discuss the graphic devices you've plugged in and solicit their ideas.

This is also the time to work on the design of any enclosures going with the letter: coupons, certificates, product photos, or reply cards. Whatever you select, be absolutely certain that you like it and that it appeals to your target readers. Changes after this stage are expensive and frustrating. Think twice.

STEP 22: Edit Again

Oops! Did you mean to write that? Wasn't the page break supposed to come farther down the sheet? Why did you choose to print the text in that hard-to-read color? What did you have in mind when you chose that typeface? Why is the headline hardly distinguishable from the rest of the letter?

This is a painful step. Nobody likes it. But you will notice things to change in this supposedly finished form, things that you missed previously. Bite the bullet and make the changes. You don't want anything less than a completely compelling sales letter.

(Once you've accepted the idea of making these changes, it's probably as good a time as any to repeat Step 15, "Check the Checklists.")

STEP 23: Mail a Mockup

Things seem to be all set. It's off to the printer, right?

Wrong.

Now is the time for you to put together the best mockup of the entire mailing that you can, with all the enclosures, then mail it to yourself. Your objective here is to receive it, see it, and handle it in the context of your normal stack of mail.

This may seem like a needlessly time-consuming chore, but it is perhaps the most important of the later steps. If your piece is of such a size that it will be roughed up and damaged by the post office, you should know that. If your piece does not compare well to the other mail you receive on an average day, you should know that. If your piece is meant to convey a "personalized" feeling, and it winds up looking like the rest of the "junk mail," you should know that.

You have worked too hard and spent too much time developing your letter to send it out without determining exactly how it will appear in its actual selling environment. Take the time to produce a mockup and mail it. Your prospective customers will likely look much less charitably on the receipt of your letter than you do, but you will at least have something approaching a "real-life" test of your letter's initial appearance and effectiveness.

STEP 24: The Cool-Off

You probably don't want to hear this, but the best thing for you to do once you receive your mockup is—nothing. At least for a few days. The reason? You need to win back some objectivity. That quality is probably in pretty short supply now.

The more you work with your sales letter, the more likely you are to fall in love with it—see its beauties but not its blemishes. Also, you're going to get impatient with this admittedly lengthy—but effective—system. For these reasons, a three- to five-day cooling-off period is a good idea.

I confess that I sometimes work under such intense deadline pressure that I skip this step, even several of these last steps; I think my finished work in those situations suffers a little as a result. I would welcome the luxury of extra time to restore my objective judgment. If you have the time, take the time.

STEP 25: Get Second Opinions

I believe in getting second opinions, within certain very definite limits. You may have gotten such opinions earlier in this process, as part of pretesting. It won't hurt to get them again, now that you have done a great deal more work. The more experienced your contact, the better the advice you receive is likely to be.

Getting an Expert Second Opinion

What's an expert? Tough question. Everybody recognizes how unqualified everybody else is to opine on a matter, but no one considers himself unqualified to do so. (Consider that several surveys have shown something close to 70 percent of all licensed drivers to consider themselves "above average"—a statistical impossibility!) There is certainly no shortage of available opinions. Unfortunately, most are at best worthless and at worst dangerous.

Many people in direct marketing develop their own little networks of peers and colleagues they can bounce ideas, copy, and drafts off of in search of valid feedback. If you write a lot of sales letters, you need to develop such a network. If you don't know appropriate people, I'd suggest setting about meeting them. Seek out your local Glazer-Kennedy Insider's Circle Chapter if there is one in your area, and attend its meetings. You'll find the Glazer-Kennedy Independent Business Advisor exceptionally skilled in my kind of marketing, you'll find very astute marketers in a variety of businesses attending, and probably meet pro copywriters there too.

There are chapters in many cities and towns throughout North America. Information is available at *www.dankennedy.com* or via the free-gift offer in Part 4: Resources.

Buying an Expert Second Opinion

If you are going to do a lot of sales letter writing and want to develop your skills in this area, you may want to rent a collaborator and coach. Make an arrangement with an amenable freelance copywriter to work with you as a cowriter on a project or two, then look over your shoulder and critique your work on the next few. You might find such a helper through American Writers & Artists, at *www.awaionline.com*. They maintain a "jobs board" online, where people looking for copywriters can advertise their needs and assignments.

STEP 26: Give It the Final Review

This is it—the last chance to tinker and tighten. Take the time to find a quiet, peaceful place and scrutinize your letter just one more time.

STEP 27: Go to Press

Give it to the printers—but don't give up control. Make sure your concept stays intact. If you're dealing with a complex mailing or large quantity, check proofs and blue lines personally and carefully. Changes during this period—from the time you hand over the mechanicals to the time you give the okay for the work to go on press—fall into two categories: printer errors (PEs) and author alterations (AAs).

After following the exhaustive review and double-check procedures outlined in this book, there's very little likelihood you're going to decide to rewrite paragraphs now. But if you do, be prepared to pay—a lot. AAs are expensive, and you should only indulge in them if you find a glaring and damaging mistake. At this point, moving commas from inside the quotation marks to outside isn't the best use of your resources.

PEs, however, are another story. If you wanted yellow underlining and got a dull orange, make some noise and don't let the printer talk you into letting it go "as is." If the photos have uneven color values, tell the printer to go back and do the job again. If you selected a certain paper stock/color/size and are told it will be "easier for everybody" if you use what "everyone else uses," raise a stink about it. You're paying the bill. You're calling the shots. If the letter doesn't deliver, you will be the one to get hurt. Have it your way.

Of course, correcting PEs—errors arising from printer mistakes—should not cost you anything extra. Nevertheless, it is not uncommon for a few such items to sneak onto your bill once the job is complete. Printers do this to see if you are really paying attention. Don't let them down; show them that you are.

Chapter 10

Major-League Play

I mean no disrespect when I say that many sales letter writers and users play—and can win—in the minor leagues. Often, this means the use of sales letters directed at relatively small lists on behalf of small, local businesses, in environments where the competition is entirely unaware of effective use of sales letters. In minor-league play like this, the twenty-seven steps provided so far are more than sufficient for successful outcomes and will give you great competitive advantage.

But if your circumstances require—or you are interested in—major-league play, there are additional steps to consider. . . .

STEP 28: Test

If you are mailing a small number of letters on behalf of a local business, you may not have feasible opportunity to test different variables against each other—especially if your letter campaign is for a one 'n' done promotion. But if you are hoping to own a somewhat evergreen sales letter that can be used or reused on an ongoing basis in fairly large quantities, you will be best served by giving yourself more than one way to win. For my clients, I almost always develop a test matrix of several to many versions of the letter to split-test. Doing this with online sales letters at websites is easier and less costly, as traffic can be directed to each site in rotation, but—caution—online results are indicative but not perfectly predictive of what will happen in the mail, for a variety of reasons too numerous to detail here.

Anyway, you might test one headline versus another, one photo versus another, one offer versus another, one bonus versus another, one guarantee versus another, etc. If you think of that as a matrix then incorporate every possible variable, you can see that it gets complicated:

Headline #A with:

Photo #1

Photo #2

Offer #1 and Photo #1

Offer #1 and Photo #2

Offer #2 and Photo #1

Offer #2 and Photo #2

Photo #1 and Offer #1 and Bonus #1

Photo #1 and Offer #2 and Bonus #1

Photo #1 and Offer #1 and Bonus #2

Photo #1 and Offer #2 and Bonus #2

Etc.

. . . and again with Headline #B.

. . . and I didn't even suggest testing one format against another, and different lists or list segments.

The pros at sales letter marketing, who get rich with it, or who use it to build and fuel big companies do exactly this kind of testing. A client of mine who mails B2B in the investment industry uses photos of "hot babes"—attractive women in business attire, but sexy business attire—as attention-getting devices. In one test he found that the same woman in the same attire posed facing left versus posed facing right made a significantly measurable difference in response!

I don't imagine most people reading this book can be this sophisticated in their testing—but don't let yourself off this hook too easily. Think through the potential value of an evergreen sales letter and invest accordingly. There's a difference between being unable to test and being unwilling to test.

At the very least, you can run simple A or B, single variable split-tests almost every time you mail, and build up a bank of knowledge about what works best with your customers and prospects.

STEP 29: Sometimes, Outsourcing

When and How to Hire Pro Copywriters

It makes sense for you to have a basic understanding of how professional, freelance copywriters—pens for hire—work, because there will likely be a situation at some point in your business life when it will make good sense to move from the do-it-yourself output this book guides in to bringing in more-expert reinforcements.

There are several instances in which paying pros to do your sales copywriting makes sense.

I am usually brought in when it is a high-stakes game, such as when the client has a very high transaction size and customer value or is going to invest a large sum in direct mail or other media.

I am also often brought in when the client is launching a business with a do-or-die campaign or is competing in a very difficult environment, where his targeted consumer is being marketed to by very smart, tough competitors who are using top copywriters—or all of the above! These conditions are necessary because of my compensation requirements and preference for complex, multistep, multimedia projects. As of this writing, my typical project fees run from $100,000.00 to $2 million, plus royalties linked to results. Obviously, the local cupcake store or single dental practice has no opportunity sizeable enough to make such an investment in me, or one of the few dozen other top freelance copywriters in my league. This does not mean I work only for large corporations. The opposite is true. Eighty percent of my work is with solo entrepreneurs and small to midsize companies, often with only a few million dollars a year in revenue, who I help multiply sales and profits.

---

70 percent said they'd renewed a relationship with a business because they received its direct mail.

94 percent took action on promotional offers they received via direct mail.

40 percent tried a new business after receiving its direct mail

(Source: DM News/PitneyBowes Survey)

If the fee size sounds big to you, and you wonder why on earth anybody would pay $100,000.00 to have an ad, a sales letter, or a print campaign written for them, consider three situations. First, creation of an asset. In many cases, the work I do is used repetitively or continuously over years and not only generates millions in direct revenue but brings in customers with substantial lifetime value. So I and astute clients don't think of my work as work, as a service rendered, but as the development of a very valuable asset, akin to a building in which a factory or store operates, equipment that produces revenue, or—a good analogy—a salesman out on the hustings drumming up business, in which a salary, bonuses, health care, company car, and expense account totaling more than my fee each year must be invested. Second, big paydays. If my marketing campaign is, as example, for a big seminar or conference where each attendee is worth, say, $2,000.00, or for a chain of weight loss clinics where each patient is worth $2,000.00, then (a) $1 million or even more may be at stake in just a weekend or week, and (b) it takes small, marginal improvement with my help versus without my help to cover my cost. If there would ordinarily be 500 at the event, I need only boost that by 10 percent to earn my keep. Third, desperate circumstances, when survival in a war with competitors or turnaround of a troubled business hangs in the balance. During the recent recession (quite possibly still delaying full emergence of a healthier new economy as you read this), my office has often been a MASH unit for the wounded, injured, and bleeding in need of 9-1-1 emergency assistance!

Obviously, many businesses do not have needs or opportunities of sufficient scope and size to warrant my involvement, so less costly copywriters with skills sufficient for the less challenging tasks must exist—and they do. The other instances in which business owners find it necessary or smart to bring in outside copywriters include special, one-and-done campaigns like a grand opening or new product launch; when the business needs a lot of prolific communication with customers, including daily e-mails, monthly newsletters, etc., that the owner can't do himself; or for specific media, such as websites or social media. Many small, local businesses do find and hook up with freelance copywriters whose own fees are modest and who have better skills than the business owner is willing to develop himself. There is a good copywriter for every purpose and every budget. The best place to shop for copywriters is through American Writers & Artists. AWAI trains and develops copywriters, provides ongoing training, and functions as the professional association of freelance copywriters. More importantly for you, the client, they connect businesses looking for copywriters with writers via their own online "jobs center." You can learn more by visiting *www.awaionline.com*.

If you happen to have a business engaged in a high-stakes game that might warrant my attention, you can contact me directly by sending a brief description of your business and your needs and opportunities as you perceive them to my assistant, Vicky, via fax at 602-269-3113. She'll take it from there.

When you decide to use outside, pro copywriters, there are several key things to look for and keep in mind:

- **It is usually better—and possible—to find someone with experience specifically relevant to your type of business or clientele rather than just a competent copywriter**. The best copywriters tend to specialize in fewer than a dozen product/service categories.
- **You have to decide what you are looking for in a copywriter.** Do you want someone just to write to assignment, someone to collaborate with, or someone who functions not just as a copywriter but as a consultant and marketing strategist (as I do)?

- **You do not want to overpay but you don't want to underpay either**. You can find, for example, copywriters who'll do a four-page sales letter for $500.00, $5,000.00, $15,000.00, or $50,000.00. Which is the right fee? It depends. On many factors. You have to assess the potential value of the end product you will own. Can it be used repeatedly or continuously or is it to be used one time only? What is its purpose, and what is the value of that purpose—is it, for example, just promoting a sale to existent customers or, if B2B, is it bringing highly valuable, key new clients to your trade show booth? What level of experience and expertise is needed for success? If you are hiring a mechanic for your NASCAR pit crew, you need a different level of expertise than if hunting for a mechanic to keep your minivan in tip-top condition. It would be foolish to pay the money needed for the NASCAR guy for the family minivan care, but dumb to economize by hiring the neighborhood grease monkey for your NASCAR pit crew.

- **Be cautious of anybody too quick to agree on the assignment and race to the keyboard**. In sales copywriting, preparation is more than half the battle. You want someone who invests time in gathering information from you and from other sources, who engages in a learning curve about you and your product. Again, different levels of this are needed in different circumstances, and affordable only to certain degrees in different circumstances. You can also have significant impact on success by how much good, solid information you provide to your copywriter.

- **Avoid misunderstandings and dissatisfaction by beginning with complete clarity about the size, scope, deliverables, timelines and other details of the assignment(s) or ongoing relationship.** Most copywriters have contracts or letters of agreement, but if yours doesn't, you should insist on getting everything in writing. And, in multiproject or ongoing situations, make sure there's the equivalent of a prenuptial agreement. Determine in advance how you can end the relationship or how the copywriter can end the relationship in a manner fair to both parties.

When Should You Hire a Beginner with Little Experience?

Every writer is a beginner when beginning. I had my first client, and early clients, just like every other writer must. For the most part, mine were small, local businesses with relatively small-size opportunities (nonetheless, significant to them), where my young skills built mostly from study rather than experience could produce results, and we could agree on modest fees. My earliest clients included a wine and cheese shop, a custom bowling-ball manufacturer selling only to bowling centers, and a local ad agency that farmed out work to me. I soon found a small but very growth-oriented publishing company that I could grow with.

If yours is a very small business with limited-size opportunity and strictly limited budget, working with a relative beginner may be the only choice, and can be a very good choice. You can provide a place for the copywriter to "cut his teeth," get experience, and document successful results; you can get bargain-priced work and an exceptional degree of personal attention and time investment. You can, essentially, grow together.

To whatever degree you can afford experience, though, buy it—because legitimate, relevant experience is almost always less expensive than experimentation. When someone rents me, they get thirty-five years' experience encompassing millions of dollars of other peoples' money invested in experimentation.

Be Able to Do It, Even If You Don't

My best clients, for whom I achieve the best results, are so knowledgeable about direct response and direct marketing in general, and sales copywriting in specific, that they are perfectly capable of writing effective copy for themselves. They choose to outsource it for a variety of reasons, ranging from speed, time and time-value of money, to the belief that two heads are better than one, to a need or desire for the best possible results, not just good enough results. But because they could do it, their judgment about it is valid and valuable, their input useful, and they can be a part of the process. If you merely blindly delegate with little or no understanding of what effective sales copy is or how it is crafted, you are at the complete mercy of your hired-gun with no means of evaluating the work before spending money putting it out there, no way to make a positive contribution, and at great risk of meddling and sabotaging the work with unfounded opinions. That's why reading this book is a good thing even if you outsource all your copywriting.

Part 3

The Most Versatile Sales Tool of All

Now that you've learned the Ultimate Sales Letter System and have it at your disposal, you'll want to get the maximum value from it. There are eight major ways we can use these kinds of sales letters for our businesses and our clients. In this section, we'll look at each one.

Chapter 11

Using Sales Letters in Business

In previous chapters, you've mastered the Kennedy system for creating powerful sales letters. There are seven major ways we can use these kinds of letters for our own businesses and for clients.

1. To Create Qualified Leads

In-person cold calling has become prohibitively expensive and leads to high sales force turnover. Cold-call telemarketing is also expensive and discouraging to telemarketers. In B2B, it's still possible without restrictions, but with consumers, the Do-Not-Call List laws have shrunken the pool of prospects that can be cold-called. For all these reasons, the qualifying of prospects by cold-call telemarketing is extremely unappealing, yet salespeople need qualified leads.

Once a good sales letter is developed and proved effective in generating qualified leads for your salespeople, you have the most controllable, manageable, and predictable lead generator in existence. There are, of course, many other ways to generate leads. Trade shows or mall exhibits work, but produce huge surges of leads in a few days, not a consistent flow. Media advertising of one kind or another can be used to provide leads, but results will vary tremendously based on all sorts of uncontrollable factors: day of the week, position on a page, the television program running opposite your commercial, and so on.

A letter campaign that reliably produces, say, three leads per hundred units mailed will just about always produce at that level. The inherent variables of other media do not interfere with a letter campaign.

When someone picks up the phone and calls you in response to your sales letter, you know you've got a pretty promising prospect!

2. To Support Telemarketing

Many businesses with active outbound telemarketing operations find that sending a sales letter, then following up with the telephone call, works much better than a cold telephone call by itself. The letter paves the way. It gives the telemarketer a reason for calling. It provides the interested prospect with reference information to refer to during the conversation.

This works whether the purpose of the phone call is to make an appointment or to make a sale.

A good example of this kind of letter appears as Exhibit #24.

3. To Create Store Traffic

There's a Cadillac dealer in our area who mails a sales letter to me at least once a month, announcing some type of sale or event going on at the dealership. (I assume I'm on the list by virtue of owning a Lincoln Continental and/or living in a certain zip code.) These letters are designed to create traffic to the dealership. They are obviously working or I wouldn't keep getting them. Just about any retail business could certainly copy and use such an approach.

I know of one occasion where this kind of sales letter campaign actually built a business from scratch. A deli and restaurant targeted all of the offices and businesses nearby, including many offices in high-rise towers, and used a sales letter to reach them. I don't have access to that letter anymore, but it went something like this:

Who Says There's No Such Thing as a Free Lunch?

To introduce you to our huge, delicious sandwiches made to order with fresh deli meats and imported cheeses, we're going to give you a free lunch—no strings attached—no other purchase necessary. Come by yourself, bring the whole gang—from now until April 1, everybody gets a free sandwich!

The letter then continued with several short paragraphs describing the deli's specialty sandwiches, locations, hours, and credit cards honored.

Of course, people bought drinks, side salads, and desserts, and the profit on those items helped offset the true cost of the free sandwiches. And the owner calculated that "buying his clientele" for a couple of months this way would be faster and cheaper than a longer-term commitment to all sorts of media advertising. He was right. By the time he had mailed only 300 letters, he had given away nearly twice that many sandwiches—and satisfied enough people that his repeat business every day jammed that little restaurant to its seams.

4. To Introduce New Products or Services to Present or Past Clients

If there is one universal discovery I've made with every business I've ever consulted with—small or large, local or global, industrial or consumer-targeted, product or service-oriented—it is that they all underutilize their own customer mailing lists. (Some don't even maintain such a list!)

I have a simple premise and a simpler plan for increasing just about any business's sales through the use of sales letters. First, the premise: it is easier to sell more to customers who know you, like you, and trust you than it is to get more new customers. The first sale is the toughest; the established customer is predisposed to purchase from you again. Second, the method: develop and mail a new sales letter to all your customers each and every month, introducing a new product or service.

Let me point out, by the way, that if a product or service is new to the customer, it's new, period. I have one client who sells a variety of products to hospitals and clinics. We broke down his customer lists by what people had bought and what they hadn't bought. Even though he sells about a hundred different items, most customers were buyers of only three or four. So we created a complex program of single-product sales letters sent to nonbuyers of those products. If you bought Product A, you got a letter about a product you hadn't bought—say, Product B. But if you were a user of B and had never bought A, you got the letter about A. These letters have been consistently pulling a 2 percent to 3 percent order rate and averaging $1.00 of gross profit per letter mailed. Think about that! If every sales letter you mail reliably brings back at least $1.00 of profit, what do you do? Right—mail as many as you can!

5. To Sell Directly by Mail Order

Mail order is a huge subject in and of itself that cannot be covered here. I would only like to point out that many nonmail order firms can still generate some business purely through sales letters.

Earlier in this book I showed you how a Las Vegas hotel marketed "vacation packages" via sales letters.

If you have regular, repeat customers, there's probably a way for you to obtain reorders and stimulate additional purchases from them with periodic sales letters.

An example of an "ordinary business" using a sales letter to sell directly by mail appears as Exhibit #25.

6. To Reduce Refunds via Post-Purchase Reassurance

Salespeople are familiar with "buyer's remorse": Someone may buy something on impulse, then a day or two later begin to feel bad about the purchase. Maybe the product isn't exactly what the buyer thought it was, maybe the problem has nothing to do with the product but a lot to do with having spent the money. Regardless of the reason, buyer's remorse can lead to refunds.

A good sales letter—with a congratulatory theme—sent to the customer the day after the purchase can make the sale stick.

An example of such a letter (Exhibit #26) was developed for a self-improvement program sold via television infomercials. Use of this letter, sent separately from the product, significantly reduced returns. Couldn't the same type of letter help with any product, service, or transaction where buyer's remorse can set in?

7. For All Sorts of Business and Personal Correspondence and Communication

We spend the lion's share of our lives selling! You have to sell yourself and your ideas to superiors, subordinates, associates, stockholders, vendors, and countless others every day. Actually, very little communication takes place without the intent of persuading.

Whether you need to write a letter to a customer or a supplier, to your stockholders, to the banker, to your son's or daughter's school principal, or to your senator, you'll be attempting to sell at least a viewpoint, if not something significantly more tangible than that.

The principles behind the system, then, apply to every type of persuasive communication. Studied and used, these techniques will make you a much more effective communicator.

Exhibit #24

"A money-saving message
exclusively for
small company CEOs . . ."

Dear Beleaguered Business Owner,

I say "beleaguered" because I know you are surrounded by taxes—payroll taxes, income taxes, sales taxes, taxes, taxes and more taxes!!! Well, I have some incredibly good news for you:

In the last 6 months, right here in (name of city), our company has helped 164 businesses reduce their property taxes. We've helped more than 100 even get rebates! We believe we can do the same for you.

Best of all, there is no charge for our service—unless and until we put money in your bank account!

It will take me less than 30 minutes to . . .

1. Explain this service and our other business services to you

2. Look at just four statistics in your financial statements, to determine the probability of us saving you money

One of my associates will be calling you in the next few days to arrange an appointment that is convenient for you. Please ask your receptionist or secretary to put through the call from DOLLAR-SAVERS INC., so we can get together soon.

Thank you,

John Q. Dollar

John Q. Dollar
President
Dollar-Savers, Inc.

P.S. Remember—the sooner we get to talk to you, the sooner we can work to reduce your tax burden!

Exhibit #25

THE PET FOOD SUPERSTORE
123 Dog Street
City, State, Zip

Dear Customer,

SAVE 50% ON NEW SUPER-ANTI-TICK SHAMPOO JUST
RIGHT FOR THE COMING SUMMER SEASON

We appreciate your business; we appreciate having you as a
customer! Now, thanks to a special arrangement with the DOG
CARE PRODUCTS COMPANY, we have an opportunity to say
"Thanks!" with a very special, timely offer:

The enclosed brochure fully explains DOG CARE'S new
SUPER-ANTI-TICK SHAMPOO and ANTI-TICK COLLAR
products. You'll do your dog and your family a favor by putting
these products to use before the start of the summer tick season, in just a few weeks. Right now, you can get a ½-quart
bottle of the Shampoo and the Collar at half-price . . . you save
$9.95! . . . you pay only $9.95. And you can order by mail or
phone, and use your Visa or MasterCard if you like. We'll set the
products aside here at the store for you or we'll ship them out,
right to your door at no extra charge!

Call us today at 258-DOGG!

Your Friends At The Superstore!

Exhibit #26

Hello again!

By now you should already be deeply involved in your **THINK AND GROW RICH SUCCESS SYSTEM.** So I wanted to write and add my personal words of encouragement—and issue you a special challenge.

First, let me re-emphasize: I believe you now have the very best program of its kind in existence. By listening to the audiocassettes repeatedly (as you commute to and from work, for example), you'll find yourself automatically "getting in tune" with the thinking, the attitudes, the convictions necessary to win big in life! And by studying the book and utilizing the other course materials as directed, you'll master the principles and discover Napoleon Hill's great success secret that much sooner.

Let me also encourage you to give some time to studying your bonus **THINK AND GROW RICH** Business Reports and listening to the accompanying audiocassettes, which were prepared exclusively for you. Whether you want to start a business from scratch, buy a going business, buy a franchise, or more effectively promote your present enterprise, these reports provide "nuts and bolts" information you can put to work right now. Even if you don't yet see yourself as an entrepreneur, you can use the guidelines in the report on Winning Career Strategies to begin moving ahead. And the report entitled How to Gain Control of Your Finances may well be worth the entire price of admission!

Altogether, this system gives you a winning game plan. So now—as my coaches used to tell me—all you've got to do is execute! And that brings me to the second thing I wanted to talk with you about: the temptation to quit.

Even though this **THINK AND GROW RICH SUCCESS SYSTEM** has been wonderfully designed to help you master the principles as easily as possible, it still requires some dedication and persistent effort on your part.

Do you remember the old bromide, "Quitters never win and winners never quit?" Well, with that in mind, I'm going to say something now that may shock you: we're all quitters! And the sooner we realize it, the better. Then we can get on with the business of overcoming it.

Let me tell you about the time I quit.

It was in my next-to-last year in football, the 1977–78 season. With me as quarterback the year before, the Vikings had lost their third Super Bowl. The Minnesota fans had decided that Tarkenton had to go. People came up to me on the streets and in restaurants to tell me just that!

Our third game of the new season was against the Tampa Bay Buccaneers, then a two-year-old expansion team that had lost every game the previous year. Now they were in Minnesota playing the mighty Vikings, but we were losing in the fourth quarter!

Our great team had gotten a little older. We were struggling. In that fourth quarter, I think all 47,000 people in the stadium stood up and booed me. I'll never forget that day. I had suffered some mighty booing during my final season with the New York Giants in 1971, but nothing hurt as much as the sound of those Viking fans calling for my head on a platter. I came off the field that day more depressed and angry than I had ever been.

The next morning I walked into Coach Bud Grant's office and said, "I'm going home to Atlanta and I'm not coming back." I was quitting after the third game of the season. The next day Bud called me in Atlanta. I said, "I've thought about it and I'm still quitting."

Bud Replied, "Fran, I wish I had some magic word to tell you that would make you come back and play. But I don't. I just hope you understand that if you don't come back, we have no chance to make the playoffs this year."

Now that really hit me!

I thought to myself, "You selfish son of a gun! Here you have 44 teammates out there. Old Tinglehoff and Marshall are up there busting their backsides. They're old and tired and they're still trying. But just because you get booed, you're going to run off and throw their chances to the wolves."

After I hung up, I packed my bags, got the next plane back to Minneapolis, and never said a word to anyone. I just showed up for Wednesday practice. Most people never knew I had quit.

The important thing to recognize is that winners are people who sometimes have the desire to quit, but *they develop ways of dealing with it.* And that's what **THINK AND GROW RICH** is all about.

Why have I told you this story?

Because you'll probably be tempted to quit, too. Maybe you'll listen to the tapes for a little while and not see any miraculous changes in your life, so you'll feel like quitting. Sometimes we're a little too "instant"-oriented these days. Maybe you'll try some new venture and "get your nose bloodied," and feel like quitting. I want you to know that, as far as I'm concerned, it's perfectly okay to feel like quitting now and then—<u>as long as you don't!</u>

I really want to see you take this winning **THINK AND GROW RICH** game plan and execute! That's why I'm excited about offering you this little challenge and reward:

Whenever you're ready, send in a list of the 25 most valuable ideas you've gained from your study of this THINK AND GROW RICH SYSTEM. Tell us how you've benefited from these ideas. We'll then send you a suitable-for-framing Certificate of Completion with Dr. Napoleon Hill's picture and his famous quotation, "Anything the mind can conceive and believe, it can achieve"; my photograph; and the signatures of myself and Mr. W. Clement Stone, the president of the Napoleon Hill Foundation.

I hope you'll be proud to hang this beautiful certificate in a prominent place in your home or office, where you'll see it often and be reminded that anything <u>you</u> can conceive and believe, <u>you</u> can achieve.

In closing, let me congratulate you once again on investing in this tested and proven program of self-development and achievement.

Believe me, I meet people all the time who wish for greater success, but I meet far fewer who, like you, are willing to do something about it.

Sincerely,

Fran Tarkenton

Fran Tarkenton

P.S. I've enclosed, as an extra gift from the publisher, two 25% discount certificates. Each may be used toward the purchase of any of the other fine programs offered in the **THINK AND GROW RICH BUSINESS REPORTS.** To me, winning is a daily proposition, something you're always learning to do better. For this reason, you'll undoubtedly want to add some of these other excellent programs to your success library.

ADVANCED SALES COPY STRATEGY #5

If It Doesn't Look or Quack Like a Duck, Maybe It's Not a Duck

Sometimes the best way to get your sales letter welcomed and read with interest is for it to masquerade as something other than a sales letter. Earlier in this book I briefly mentioned several alternative formats, notably advertorials and tear-sheet mailings. But I've kept one of my all-time favorites for last: the sales letter disguised as a book. I have made fortunes with this device.

In some instances, the existence of this tool allows you to change your advertising, and offer the book instead of advertising the business. Many moons ago, I did this with a client awash in competitive clutter, a cosmetic surgeon in Beverly Hills, where everyone is, by law, either a cosmetic surgeon or patient, and there's a surgeon on every corner. In *Los Angeles Magazine*, there were pages of full-page ads for cosmetic surgery practices that all looked a lot alike and all said much the same thing. For Dr. Robert Kotler, who you may have seen recently on the TV show *Dr. 90210*, we changed from advertising his practice to advertising his book, *The Consumer's Guide to Cosmetic Surgery*. This instantly separated him from all the other advertisers, elevated his status as expert/celebrity author, and offered more opportunities for prospective patients to respond to than scheduling an appointment. When put in prospective patients' hands, the book was taken more seriously, given more credibility, and read more thoroughly than any fancy brochure. I have since used this tactic and tool myself and for countless clients, with great success.

My friend Nigel Worrall is in the business of renting very nice homes in central Florida as everything-included vacation homes. You can see his business at *http://floridaleisure.com*.

He uses three sales letters disguised as books, each brilliantly prepared. Two are aimed at owners of properties and investors, one at vacationers who are interested in renting a home.

Nigel can advertise these books instead of his services. He can put them in peoples' hands by themselves or accompanied by other sales letters or literature. When people request or buy a book, they are much more likely to read it than they are a sales letter per se, that they prejudge as offering no useful or interesting information. They are even a bit obligated to read a book given them, because it has perceived value and was obviously invested in. This is a terrific way to deliver a disguised sales message!

Exhibit #27

Florida Vacation Home Owners:

5 BIG MISTAKES TO AVOID
WHEN SELECTING A PROPERTY MANAGEMENT COMPANY

By Nigel G. Worrall

Exhibit #28

WHAT YOU NEED TO KNOW ABOUT

RENTING A FLORIDA VACATION HOME

By Nigel G. Worrall

Chapter 12

The Million-Dollar Sales Letter Secret: The Power of a Sequence

One of the biggest mistakes most marketers make is doing "one-shot mailings." Simply put, it takes repetition to have impact. But I advise against Madison Avenue's extraordinarily slow, patient, plodding, expensive version of repetition, with results sloppily measured by market-share movement or brand recognition over long periods of time. Instead, I most often work with a tight, timed sequence over a forty-five- to sixty-day period, capable of quickly creating brand/message recognition as well as considerable, immediate response.

In this section, I've reprinted a series of my sales letters (Exhibits #29 and #30) for a chain of Italian restaurants that has literally become famous; I've used it in all my seminars for nearly twenty years and shown it to well over 4 million people. For years, the only way to get this "model" was in my Magnetic Marketing System, for $399.00 or more. Not only do these letters include many of the tactics presented throughout this book, but they demonstrate how to structure a multistep mailing sequence. After you read these sample letters, ask yourself this simple question: do you have any doubt that, in any household receiving these letters, Giorgio's is not a topic of conversation?

Of course, people who sell "sophisticated" stuff to "sophisticated" people will quickly insist they could never use something like this. They're very wrong. You *can* separate style from structure. The humorous style helps whether selling million-dollar computer systems to CEOs in the boardroom or carpet cleaning to folks in their living rooms. But the structure is absolutely proven to be universally effective. Often, the response from the second and third letters combined will double the response obtained from the first. Sometimes, even better.

I call this my "million-dollar secret" because the creation of sales letter *sequences* rather than just creating sales letters is as responsible as any other, single idea for my becoming a millionaire while still young enough to enjoy it, and for making millions and millions of dollars for my personal clients. As secrets go, I suppose it's not much of one. Frankly, I "stole" it from the collection industry; the Giorgio's letters, for example, are very closely modeled after a basic sequence of dunning letters—first notice, second notice, third notice. But very, very few marketers know to use this tactic or have the discipline to use it, so it's just as valuable as a bona fide secret.

Appointment, No Sale

Many businesses and professional practices, from the auto dealership to the chiropractic practice, have people come in for sales presentations but leave without buying. All too often, the belief of salespeople and managers alike is "there are no Be-Backs," meaning if we let them get away, we can't get them back to buy later. It is an entirely false and very, very costly belief. I have routinely used the steps presented to you in this book to craft follow-up sales letter sequences to such nonbuyers and gotten from 10 percent to 30 percent to return and buy what they initially said no to, within days to weeks.

Exhibit #29

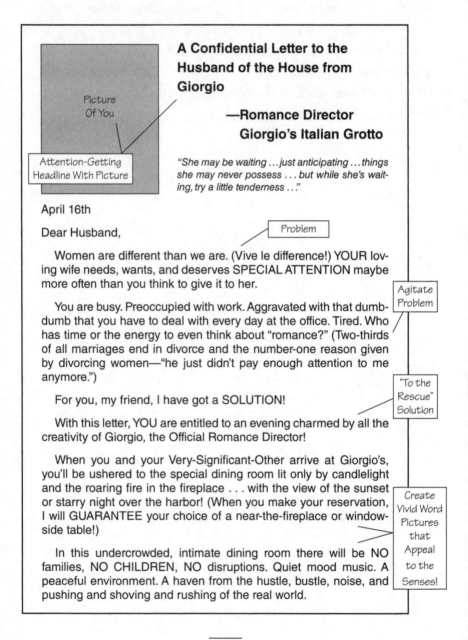

Picture Of You

Attention-Getting Headline With Picture

A Confidential Letter to the Husband of the House from Giorgio

—Romance Director Giorgio's Italian Grotto

"She may be waiting ... just anticipating ... things she may never possess ... but while she's waiting, try a little tenderness ..."

April 16th

Dear Husband,

Problem

Women are different than we are. (Vive le difference!) YOUR loving wife needs, wants, and deserves SPECIAL ATTENTION maybe more often than you think to give it to her.

Agitate Problem

You are busy. Preoccupied with work. Aggravated with that dumb-dumb that you have to deal with every day at the office. Tired. Who has time or the energy to even think about "romance?" (Two-thirds of all marriages end in divorce and the number-one reason given by divorcing women—"he just didn't pay enough attention to me anymore.")

For you, my friend, I have got a SOLUTION!

"To the Rescue" Solution

With this letter, YOU are entitled to an evening charmed by all the creativity of Giorgio, the Official Romance Director!

When you and your Very-Significant-Other arrive at Giorgio's, you'll be ushered to the special dining room lit only by candlelight and the roaring fire in the fireplace ... with the view of the sunset or starry night over the harbor! (When you make your reservation, I will GUARANTEE your choice of a near-the-fireplace or window-side table!)

Create Vivid Word Pictures that Appeal to the Senses!

In this undercrowded, intimate dining room there will be NO families, NO CHILDREN, NO disruptions. Quiet mood music. A peaceful environment. A haven from the hustle, bustle, noise, and pushing and shoving and rushing of the real world.

On your table, in a crystal bud vase, there will be a single dewy-fresh red rose for your lady. (It and the vase are hers to take home.)

We will begin with a carafe of our wonderful house Italian wine—red or white, your choice—compliments of Giorgio! And fresh baked, piping hot, lightly garlic-buttered, crusty Italian breadsticks.

For dinner, all the TENDERNESS the two of you can handle—if you choose the specialty of the house: an entrée of melt-in-your-mouth tender veal on a bed of angel hair pasta, with a to-die-for pesto sauce . . . or your choice of five other wonderful entrees.

Any choice from our dessert tray . . .

> Really Make Them See, Smell, and Taste It!

Espresso . . .

And finally a heart-shaped box with four delicate, Italian gelato filled chocolates presented to your lady with a flourish!

Now, is that an evening to enjoy, to luxuriate in, to remember? Will that make you a hero? Ah—Giorgio GUARANTEES it.

We can only accommodate twelve couples each evening with this very special Romance Dinner, so it's important to call and make reservations as early as you can. Ask for me—Giorgio—Noon to 10:00 p.m. (or stop in for our Businessman's lunch). See me, and make these Romance arrangements personally. I'm the handsome-looking devil in the deep blue tuxedo jacket, in the lounge.

Awaiting your commands—to make 'a magic for you!

> Limited Number Available

Giorgio.

P.S. The cost? EVERYTHING, the entire Romance Dinner for two exactly as I've described it—just $59.95. If you wish you can even pay in advance with VISA, MASTERCARD, AMERICAN EXPRESS, or CARTE BLANCHE and not be troubled by a check the evening you are here.

Exhibit #30

Picture
Of You

Attention-Getting
Headline With Picture

"Three coins in the fountain . . ."

Gimmick

April 24th

Dear Husband,

As you can see, I've attached 3 shiny pennies to this letter. I've done this for two important reasons: first, to grab your attention for just a moment or two or three. Second, to remind you of that wonderful romantic song "Three Coins in the Fountain . . ."

Problem

You see, this is your second notice . . . your romance wake-up call from me, Giorgio!, the Romance Director at Giorgio's Italian Grotto. My bell tolls—does it toll for thee?

It is a stress-filled, busy, hectic, tough, tiring, demanding, mind-numbing, energy-sapping battle each and every day out there, isn't it? I know—after all, I am a businessman too. (And a husband too—married to my beautiful Isabella for 25 years.) It is easy, temping, even natural to come home to "the cave" after a day of doing battle, shove the rock onto the doorway, and collapse onto the couch. BUT WITHOUT FREQUENT ROMANCE, THE FLAME FLICKERS AND DIES. You know that, deep-down inside—but who has the time and energy to create romance?

Giorgio to the rescue!!!

Agitate Problem

You know, I am deeply disappointed that I didn't hear from you after my first letter and invitation to let me create a truly romantic, memorable evening for you and your lady. So, I am here again, this time with an EVEN BETTER INVITATION . . . a truly remarkable offer . . .

For just $59.95, I will give you everything I described before, the romantic Dinner For Two—listed again, at the bottom of this letter—AND I WILL EVEN SEND A "STRETCH," GLEAMING WHITE, FULLY-EQUIPPED LIMOUSINE RIGHT TO YOUR HOME to pick YOU—the "Prince" and your "Princess" up—and bring you home at the end of the evening! (Imagine the look in her eyes when you walk out the door and, instead of going to the garage, your tuxedoed chauffeur steps forward and opens the door of the limousine for your lady to enter!)

Irresistible Offer

If you say "no" to this invitation—ah, is there no romance in your heart? How can this be?

Call ME, Giorgio!, right now. I'm ready to make 'a magic for you!

Giorgio.
With a song in his heart.

HERE IS EVERYTHING INCLUDED FOR THE INCREDIBLE LOW PRICE OF JUST $59.95:

Chapter 13

"High-Tech" Sales Letters

When I wrote the first edition of this book in 1990, very few marketers were using broadcast fax or fax on demand, and all the tools and media of the Internet were unknowns. Today, of course, online media is of major importance, and I've invited a leading expert on Internet marketing and writing copy for the web to contribute ideas in this section. I have two cautionary notes: one, resist the temptation to abandon the most reliable and relied-on sales and marketing tool, the sales letter delivered offline, in favor of online media. Doing so is, bluntly, slothful and stupid. For most businesses, the best current strategy is integration of online/offline and offline/online. Two, resist the temptation to think that different media alters the rules of selling at a distance. It does not. The same ingredients that make offline sales letters work make online sales letters work, as well as TV infomercials, and every other advertising deliverable. Yes, there are nuanced differences. But any abandonment of the fundamentals of what makes sales copy produce results is a grievous mistake.

> ## Writing Sales Letters That Can Sell Online
> By Rebecca Matter
> Founder, Wealthy Web Writer

We all know that copy is king . . . and that a well-crafted sales letter can boost sales, attract new customers, and encourage current customers to buy more . . . regardless of whether they're reading it online or off.

But, when we mindfully take into consideration how the online reader differs from the offline reader, we're able to greatly improve our chances of getting them to take the action we want, before leaving the website . . . and most likely never returning again.

And it's those details that give us a huge advantage over competing messages online.

You see, the fundamentals of persuasive writing remain as true online as they do for offline formats like direct mail.

The difference lies in the readers' intention and state of being when they first stumble upon your letter.

Think about it for a second.

You walk down to your mailbox to pick up the mail. You go back inside your house, close the door, and begin flipping through the stack, sorting it into piles. Magazines . . . catalogs . . . bills . . . direct mail . . .

But wait, one of those final letters catches your eye. The envelope is literally speaking to you!

So you take it, go into the living room, sit down on your sofa, open it up and start reading. You're relaxed. You've decided the letter is worth reading. There are no distractions. It's just you and the letter.

Now picture yourself sitting at your desk.

You're checking out how your stocks did today, reading an e-mail from your best friend, and looking for the best deal on flights for your upcoming vacation.

You're active ... you're task oriented ... and you're surrounded by distractions from your e-mail inbox to the banners and links that are just begging for you to click them.

It's right then that you stumble across an ad that catches your eye. You click on it, immediately arriving at a sales letter. You're already feeling impatient ... you've got a lot of other things to do online at this very moment. Is there *really* something here you need?

Oh, look, Expedia has a sale on flights. . . .

Click . . . you're gone. And you won't be back.

So while yes, the fundamentals of writing a persuasive sales letter that gets someone to buy are the same, there are a few key differences that you'll want to pay close attention to when crafting an online sales letter.

And I'm going to give you my five best tips for improving the results of each and every online sales letter you write.

Wealthy Web Writer Tip #1: Know Your Audience

More specifically, know how prospects got to your online sales letter. That's right—I'm not talking about their age, their sex, or what their core desires and fears are at this point. If you're writing sales letters, you should already know that.

I'm talking about how your prospect—the reader—found your online sales letter.

Was he searching Google for something specific and ran across your website? Did he click on a pay-per-click ad that offered to solve his problem? Or did you direct him to it from an e-mail you sent him personally?

The key here is to consider whether or not your reader was searching to solve a problem when he came to your sales letter or if you were the one who identified that need and then offered to fix it. The result will impact the way you speak to the readers once they've arrived.

If they find you while searching for a solution, they're looking for something and will want to know immediately *if* you can help them . . . if you have anything to offer them.

But if you lead them to the sales letter, with an e-mail for example, they *know* you can help them, but they're now looking for the proof and waiting for you to convince them why they should stay instead of clicking their mouse to escape.

Think about this and write to that person accordingly. And remember, one of the biggest benefits of writing an online sales letter is that you can have as many versions as you need!

Wealthy Web Writer Tip #2: Get Those Big Benefits Front and Center

"Sell the sizzle . . . not the steak," said Elmer Wheeler, Master Salesman. I'm sure you've heard that one a million times before—you sell with benefits not with features. But just to make sure we're on the same page, I'll illustrate with a quick example.

Say your reader is looking online for a diet plan that will help her lose twenty pounds by summer. When writing your sales letter, you won't focus your copy on the fact that the diet program includes seven patented supplements that she'll take daily. That's a feature, which you'll mention, but in all honesty she couldn't really care less about that. You'll focus on what losing those twenty pounds will do for her . . . how it will make her feel. She'll feel confident in her bikini and heads will turn to look at her when she walks across the beach. That's the benefit of your diet.

Selling with benefits is one of the first things most copywriters learn, and one of the most important elements of an effective sales letter. And while with an online sales letter they're equally important, it's the placement of those benefits that differs. People reading online are often more impatient, and easily distracted. You need to pay close attention to what appears "above the fold," which refers to the area you can see on a website without having to scroll down. When writing an online sales letter, make sure you get some of your biggest benefits into that area.

With an offline sales letter, once readers have sat down to read it, you can easily get them to read the first full page or two, but that's not the case online. You only have a couple of paragraphs to grab them and convince them not to click away. So make sure they know the benefits of what you're offering them right up front.

Wealthy Web Writer Tip #3: Pay Attention to Layout and Design

Now, this tip is going to include a lot of little tips all rolled into one. Think of this tip as a crash course into effective web design, with only one objective in mind: Make the page as easy to read as possible.

There are so many reasons why your readers can and most likely will leave your online sales letter before they finish reading it. It's the nature of the beast. . . . It's the Internet.

Remember what we talked about earlier: they're not sitting on the couch. They're not relaxed. They're not committed. *Anything* that distracts them or makes it hard to read will cause them to leave. So we need to keep them focused and lead them to our call to action.

Ready for your crash course? Let's dive in.

1. Get rid of any and all distractions. Remove pointless links. Bottom line: If it doesn't help the reader get to the call to action, get rid of it.
2. Write your sales letter in a single column. It's been tested again and again and is proven to be easier to read, which means you have a better chance of controlling your reader's eyes and attention.
3. Pay attention to the column width. The wider the width, the harder it is to read. If it's too wide—meaning your eyes tire when traveling from the last word on one line to the first word on the next—increase the margins on either side of the sales letter to make it narrower.

4. Choose a font size that's large enough for everyone to read.

5. Don't let your designers convince you to use colored fonts or write anything in reverse (white font on black background). Even though they will often feel it "looks cool," you want your readers to be able to easily read your sales letter. Stick to black text on a white background.

6. Use shorter sentences and paragraphs online. Along with looking less intimidating, they're much easier to read and comprehend online.

7. Use subheads and bullets often, and keep them full of benefits. While this tip is relevant to both online and offline sales letters, they're needed even more online.

Remember, people reading online are impatient, and a higher percentage of them will scan rather than reading every word. So make sure you're able to keep them engaged and on the path to your call to action.

Bonus Tip: Use this as a checklist the next time you write an online sales letter!

Wealthy Web Writer Tip #4: Give Special Attention to Your Call to Action

Congratulations! You've kept your reader engaged all the way to the end. Now all you have to do is get him to *take* the action you've been leading him to all along.

You should already know what you want him to do at this point, but how you ask him to do it is what's critical.

Word choice matters here. You'll want to be specific, so first think about where the reader is in the buying process:

- Is she ready to buy? Have her "order now."
- Is he signing up for an event? Tell him to "register now."
- Is she not quite sold at this point? Let her "add to shopping cart" so you can follow up with her if she leaves before completing the sale.

The point is to really think about the action you want the reader to take, and then specifically and succinctly tell him to do it.

Finally, put the call to action within the body of your e-mail, like this:

Order right now and save $200.00.

As well as with an image like this:

> Order Now and Save $200.00!

Whatever you do, make sure your online reader can easily take the action you want, whether he's reading the entire letter word for word, or scanning the page. If he makes it to the end, there's a good chance he's looking to take action.

Wealthy Web Writer Tip #5: Revise, Test, Repeat

Things are changing all the time online. So when it comes to your online sales letter, you'll never have a final draft. And thanks to the ability to easily make changes without having to pay for a new print run, you're able to test various elements of your sales letter any time you want.

Not sure what to revise? Ask yourself these questions:

- What new ways are driving visitors to your sales letter? Did you just implement a new pay-per-click or social media campaign?
- What new needs and desires do your customers have that are leading them to your sales letter? In other words, what are they searching for?
- What pages on your website or other people's websites are now linking to your sales letter that weren't before?

Think of your sales letter as an athlete. You're trying to make him bigger, better, and faster. So you tweak the training here, add a supplement there. Does he perform better? Great, what else can you do?

Closing Thoughts

You now have the basic online copywriting techniques that will help you put together an effective online sales letter. The key is to remember that while the people reading your online and offline sales letter may be the same, the manner in which they read it, and the attitude they have, can differ greatly.

Your job with an online sales letter is to control your readers' attention so that you can get them to your call to action. And you'll do that by telling them right up front they are in the right place, and then by ensuring the path is clear.

Part 4

Resources

<u>not</u> the end.

You now have my *Ultimate Sales Letter System*. But it is only one toolkit in a whole garage of smart, sophisticated, proven, profitable advertising, marketing, sales, and success tools I'd like to invite you to use as your own ... and I'd like you to come and "play" in the garage, with access to everything, free, to then judge for yourself whether this book should end our working relationship or begin it.

As the owner of this book, you are entitled to free trial membership in Glazer-Kennedy's Insider's Circle™, including my *No B.S. Marketing Letter*, a series of fast-track business improvement webinars, other online resources, and much more. In total, at publishers' price value, there are more than $500.00 of resources waiting for you—free. To claim your gifts and activate your trial membership or to get more information, visit:

www.dankennedy.com/salesletter/gifts

Offer subject to change. Details of current offer posted at above-noted website.

Other Books by the Author

The Ultimate Marketing Plan. Adams Media, Avon, MA, 2011—companion to this book

No B.S. Series

No B.S. Business Success in the New Economy. Entrepreneur Press, Irvine, CA, 2009.

No B.S. Sales Success in the New Economy. Entrepreneur Press, Irvine, CA, 2009.

No B.S. Wealth Attraction in the New Economy. Entrepreneur Press, Irvine, CA, 2010.

No B.S. Marketing to the Affluent. Entrepreneur Press, Irvine, CA, 2008.

No B.S. Ruthless Management of People & Profits. Entrepreneur Press, Irvine, CA, 2008.

No B.S. Time Management for Entrepreneurs. Entrepreneur Press, Irvine, CA, 2004.

Making Them Believe: The 21 Principles and Lost Secrets of Dr. J. R. Brinkley-Style Marketing, with Chip Kessler. Glazer-Kennedy Publishing, New York, NY, 2010.

Uncensored Sales Strategies, with Sydney Biddle Barrows. Entrepreneur Press, Irvine, CA, 2009

Make 'Em Laugh & Take Their Money: On Using Humor as a Speaker, Writer or Sales Professional. Glazer-Kennedy Publishing, New York, NY, 2010.

The New Psycho-Cybernetics, with Dr. Maxwell Maltz. Prentice-Hall, Upper Saddle River, NJ, 2002.

Information available at *www.NoBSBooks.com*

Resources from Experts
You Met in This Book

Katie Yeakle
American Writers & Artists, Inc.
www.awaionline.com

American Writers & Artists (AWAI) offers a wide range of online courses, home study courses, training, coaching, and online community support for professional and aspiring freelance copywriters as well as in-house copywriters—those writing sales copy for their own companies.

AWAI is also a matchmaker for business owners who need professional copywriters or copywriting coaches to assist them and professional copywriters.

Mike Capuzzi
CopyDoodles®

Mike is not only the inventor/developer of CopyDoodles®, but a skilled freelance copywriter and marketing consultant, and a dynamic speaker on advertising and marketing subjects. Information about Mike is available at *www.copydoodles.com*. Information about CopyDoodles®, including a special offer for readers of this book, can be found at *www.copycosmetics.com*.

Rebecca Matter
Wealthy Web Writer

Wealthy Web Writer's website contains articles, how-to-videos, and online training videos that teach you how to write better and more profitable web copy. From online sales letters and websites, to e-mail, blogs, and social media, everything you need can be found in one place. Learn more by going to *www.wealthy webwriter.com/dankennedy*.

And once there you'll be able to sign up for a free six-part training series which will show you step-by-step how to make eleven changes to your website that will immediately improve your conversions.

Index

About the Author

Dan S. Kennedy is one of the highest-paid, most sought-after direct-response copywriters in America, specializing in sales letters commanding fees from $50,000.00 to $2 million plus royalties for copywriting projects. He is a multimillionaire, serial entrepreneur, strategic advisor, and business coach influencing over 1 million business owners annually, and the author of numerous business books, including *No B.S. Sales Success in the New Economy*. He has helped thousands of entrepreneurs make sales letters work as a driving force for their diverse businesses, from the small, local shop to billion dollar corporations.